ADULT DYSLEXIA

UNLEASHING YOUR LIMITLESS POWER

CHERYL ISAACS

B.A (Hons), M.Sc, C.Psychol, AFBPsS
Chartered & Registered Psychologist
Neurodiversity Specialist

Understanding and Using Your Dyslexia
and Neurodiversity for Maximum Success

This publication contains the opinions and ideas of its author. It is intended to provide helpful and informative material on the subjects addressed in the publication. It is sold with the understanding that the author and publisher are not engaged in rendering medical, health or any other kind of personal or professional services in the book. The reader should consult his or her medical health, or other competent professional before adopting any of the suggestions in the book or drawing inferences from it. The author and publisher specifically disclaim all responsibility for any liability, loss, or risk, personal or otherwise, which is incurred, directly or indirectly, of the use and applications of any of the contents of this book.

This book is for Sharon Buckingham,
never forgotten and always in my heart.

Acknowledgements

Special thanks to:

My wonderful family: Allen, Dad, Ray, Taz and Martin – *for always being proud of me and encouraging everything I've ever done.*

My wonderful mum, Tina Isaacs – *for saying what you said to me as a child. Your support has inspired me for life.*

Lara Sutherland – *for the constant support, use of your house when writing and the endless cups of tea and love.*

Jonathan Kemp – *for the brainstorming and detailed proof-reading!*

Steve Kelsey – *for the most inspirational short coaching session ever (which encouraged me to get this book back on track!)*

Chris Berry – *for always believing in me unequivocally, from start to finish.*

ADULT DYSLEXIA

UNLEASHING YOUR LIMITLESS POWER

Contents

Who Is This Book For?

Is this you?

Typical comments I often hear from my clients include:

 'I can remember journeys I went on when I was 7 years old, but I can't remember a phone call I took 3 minutes ago.'

 'Once I've learnt the information, I can talk about the job until the proverbial cows come home but I find it really hard to initially read something that would take my colleagues a few hours!'

 'My boss doesn't believe that I'm dyslexic because I can spell really well, but she doesn't understand why I can't organise myself.'

 'I can have a 5-minute conversation with my boss and know exactly what I am expected to do and even have ideas of how I might approach it, but by the time I walk 2 minutes back to my desk it has completely gone.'

 'When I learn something new, I am often one of the first people to understand the idea and can talk about it with my peers but when I have to write it down, I can't seem to get the ideas out of my head or structure it and when I eventually do, it takes me so much longer than others.'

If so, read on!

I was determined to produce a book specifically **for people with dyslexia and neurodiversity.** Most of the books out there are written for practitioners like me and not for people who actually have dyslexia or neurodiversity. Most clients who are assessed for dyslexia then go and buy a few books on the subject, soon to realise that they are the most boring exploration of the subject ever and not accessible at all. I wanted to do something a little different and write something solely for you.

This book is primarily **for adults.** Most of the books out there are either for practitioners or for the *parents* of dyslexic children. It's as if it all magically disappears at 18 years old! We know that adults with dyslexia tend to have different difficulties in the workplace (not necessarily reading and spelling), so I wanted to focus on other issues, not just these.

Not Neuro-diverse?

Even if you're not dyslexic, dyspraxic or neuro-diverse, the lessons to be learned from this field are still fascinating, as ultimately, we are still talking about how the brain works, the ways people learn and the really useful things to know about ourselves that help us grow in confidence. Surely that's a useful journey for everyone.

What Is This Book About?

I wanted to write a book that was **practical and useful.** I have read too many books on the subject that delve into every academic theory or model of dyslexia and are great for academic research, but do not give the **tools, ideas and understanding** that are so often being sought by my clients. I have limited the theory to the really interesting parts so that you can just focus on what you can actually do about it.

Most importantly, however, I wanted to focus on the **psychological impact of dyslexia and neurodiversity** and enable all those very intelligent people like you (yes, you), to take control of any weaknesses, understand them and live a life that allows you to be equally confident with all your lovely strengths.

In my experience, **the only difference between clients who are struggling and really successful clients is the *execution of finely tuned habits*** that allow the utilisation of strengths whilst diminishing the effects of weaknesses. For example, having a well-developed plan for comprehension when reading such as the QSR method as seen in Chapter 10 or the meeting template in the Memory chapter (Chapter 6) for taking notes. These can make a significant difference to retention and only take a few more minutes out of your day to execute.

Aims of This Book

After reading this book, you will be armed with the following knowledge:

- Your strengths and weaknesses

- Ways of viewing intelligence

- How the brain works – cognitive abilities and the latest neuroscience research

- How others experience dyslexia through real-life case studies

- Personality differences and how these will affect how you think, work and react

- How you can utilise your brain to its full potential

- How to grow your confidence and personal impact

- How to continually develop yourself

- A new insight from a psychologists' perspective

Part 1

Understanding Me

Chapter 1

Starting with a Strengths Mindset

'Men are not disturbed by things but by the view they take of them.'

Epictetus

Changing Mindsets

When I assess clients for dyslexia or any neurodiversity ('neuro' meaning 'brain', 'diversity' meaning 'difference') the first question I am often asked is 'What if this just shows I'm stupid?' Whilst I find it incredibly sad that society has led them to feel that an assessment will show some underlying flaw or inadequacy, I also feel incredibly honoured to be in the position to show them something very different about themselves.

So, let's deal with this now. **You are not stupid. In fact, you are likely to be very clever.** You just may not know it yet. What you have is uniquely brilliant and only you have it. Every single person reading this book has their own specific skill set, their own individual preferences and yes, their weaknesses too – so wonderfully imperfect.

Armed with the knowledge of **your unique strengths, weaknesses and potential developmental areas, you can achieve amazing things.**

You just need to have that knowledge. I have worked with thousands of people who had no idea how much potential lay inside of them and how this can be used to bring more quality and success to their lives.

So far, I have spent my career helping people identify and understand their inner strengths and weaknesses. What I know (for a fact) is that assessed or perceived weaknesses in literacy, spelling, writing or other common factors that can affect learning such as short-term memory, do not make you unintelligent. It is amazing how quickly even very intelligent people can be made to feel stupid over something like time-management or inbox overload!

As a psychologist, I know that most of you reading this will not have confidence in your strengths yet. Worse still, some may believe that they don't even have any defining strengths. I would just ask one thing. Stay with me for the duration. See what you can learn. And complete a few of the *Reflectors* along the way. (Reflectors are short questions designed to help you analyse the information from a personal perspective.) It is important that you build up a true picture of yourself as you go along and that you use the ideas in this book to set out a way forward that is tailored to you.

What this book doesn't do is just say things like 'be more confident' or 'you have inner power'. You have heard that enough. I hate all of that schmaltzy stuff myself. I'm going to walk you through a range of different areas so that you can understand yourself through a wider lens than just the dyslexic focus. My goal is to give you some really good ideas and some helpful, practical tools to put them into action. What I promise you is that I won't just say things like 'improve your writing confidence' or 'stay organised when learning'. This kind of advice always makes me want to scream 'Yes, but how? Give me something practical!' I am sure you've also had this experience.

Dyslexia/Neurodiversity or Just a Different Thinker

'Neurodiversity' is simply the idea of neurological differences in the brain being a result of normal variations that should be respected as any other variation. If you're reading this, then you probably consider yourself to have neuro-differences.

Dyslexia falls under the umbrella of neurodiversity and typically presents with difficulties in literacy and cognitive weaknesses in working memory.

Dyspraxia is another neuro-difference which presents with difficulties in coordination and organisation and may also show cognitive weaknesses in processing speed.

Neurodiversity is a helpful term as it accepts that there is not 'one way of thinking'. Some people have a greater memory. Some have better visual skills. Some process information faster. Some analyse data faster. Some are better with people, whereas some are better with technology. Some are more creative than others. As a group, we humans are a neuro-diverse melting pot. This has helped us from an evolutionary point of view to cover all of our requirements and to ensure that we have everything we need as a species. You just need to know which part of the ingredients you are!

The 10%ers – Famous People With Dyslexia

Did you know that 10% of the population are dyslexic? (British Dyslexia Association). The following people are great examples of what happens when you, the person with dyslexia, focus on your dyslexic strengths and not weaknesses.

- Elon Musk – Billionaire and Entrepreneur
- Richard Branson – Entrepreneur
- Dominic O'Brien – World Memory Champion
- Walt Disney – Film Producer
- Tom Cruise – Actor
- Benjamin Zephaniah – Poet
- Sir Jackie Stewart – Racing Driver
- Muhammed Ali – Boxer
- Ingvar Kamprad – Ikea Founder
- Darcey Bussell – Dancer
- Jim Carrey – Actor
- Albert Einstein – Scientist
- Lord Sugar – Entrepreneur
- Keira Knightley – Actress
- Ben Elton – Comedian
- John Lennon – Singer
- Orlando Bloom – Actor
- Theo Paphitis – Entrepreneur
- Steven Spielberg – Director
- Keanu Reeves – Actor

- David Bailey – Photographer

- Whoopi Goldberg – Actor

- Noel Gallagher – Singer

- Lara Flynn Boyle – Actress

- Robin Williams – Actor

- Magic Johnson – Basketball Player

- Eddie Izzard – Comedian

- Erin Brockovich – Socio-Environmental Activist

- Anderson Cooper – Presenter

- David Rockefeller – Businessman and Philanthropist

- Paloma Faith – Singer

I think you would agree that all of these people have been quite successful so far! They have simply known that to be their best, they would have to focus on their strengths and develop strategies for their weaknesses.

Strengths Reflector

Task: Let the journey begin! It's time to start 'understanding you'.

- Spend a few minutes considering the following question.
- Don't over-analyse and don't think about what you would *like* your strengths to be, but just what you *know* them to be.
- Start with what are you sure about, or what have people told you.

This is a useful exercise to get you into a 'strengths mindset'. In my experience, most people never think about this and that is clearly not a good thing for our confidence!

What are my top 3 strengths?
For example:

1) Interpersonal skills – talking to others and forming good relationships.

2) Creativity – coming up with new ideas and different approaches to problems.

3) Analysing information – spotting links and trends

1)

2)

3)

Strengths Research

Two years ago, I conducted some research for a webinar I was presenting for my own company. We surveyed over 100 people and asked them what they considered to be their top strengths. This is what we found.

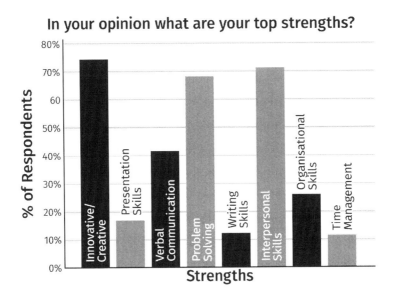

In your opinion what are your top strengths?

It is clear that people with dyslexia commonly see innovation, creativity, problem-solving and interpersonal skills as their key strengths. I often wonder what workplaces would look like if we really utilised these strengths instead of being distracted by or focusing on weaknesses.

Adapting Your Brain – Neuroplasticity

Did You Know?
It was previously thought that our brain's abilities stayed consistent

throughout life and that the brain was more or less 'fixed'. However, we now know from the field of neuroscience that brains evolve and change throughout life – this process is called **neuroplasticity** ('neuro' meaning 'brain' and 'plasticity' meaning 'change') and means the ability to shape and change according to the environment and its needs.

A brilliant example of this research was a study conducted with London taxi drivers which found they tended to have a larger hippocampus than the average person (the part which deals with memory and learning). This part of the brain had physically enlarged in order to deal with the vast amount of visual memory required for driving around the city streets. What this teaches us is that **our brains evolve and adapt if we practice tasks every day or make them a habit.**

Carol Dweck, a U.S. psychologist, has conducted some great research looking at what our brains do when we believe our intelligence is fixed (the 'fixed' mindset) compared to when we believe we can adapt and grow through persistence and effort (the 'growth' mindset). The results were astonishing. When given a difficult challenge, the group who were taught a 'growth mindset' consistently showed significantly more activation in the brain compared to the groups who were told that intelligence was 'fixed'. It appears the growth state encouraged people to seek the answer instead of giving up as easily as the other group.

The fixed mindset group showed no additional electrical activity in the brain as they assumed they could not solve the problem if they did not get results early on. *The power of the mind!*

People clearly have different strengths and weaknesses, as we will see in the next chapter, but sometimes it is useful to question if we have fully exhausted our strategies and whether we have made some assumptions about abilities which may be holding us back.

Chapter 2

What Is It?
Dyslexia and Neurodiversity Explained

'To be yourself in a world that is constantly trying to make you something else, is the greatest accomplishment.'

– *Ralph Waldo Emerson*

What Do We Mean by Dyslexia and Neurodiversity?

As a psychologist assessing dyslexia and neurodiversity, I have noticed
that people have the idea that they're going to come along to the
assessment and be tested on spelling, reading and writing under exam-
like conditions for several hours. No wonder people don't want to do
it! In reality, my clients are often quite pleased (and relieved) to know
it's not like that at all. Whilst we do look at literacy skills, one of the
most important things we do in an assessment is to look at cognitive
abilities. Cognitive abilities are simply the brain-based skills we need
to carry out any task.

In this chapter, I am going to talk generally about the four main
areas of cognitive ability so that you become familiar with the terms.
In Chapter 3, we take a deeper dive and discuss some of the research

around each of these and how they affect how you learn and work.

The four main ability areas are:

Verbal Comprehension –understanding and processing language and the ability to use language to express your thoughts – e.g., using a wide range of vocabulary to express yourself and reason verbally.

Perceptual Reasoning – the ability to use non-verbal reasoning to apply abstract logic to solve problems– e.g., putting a wardrobe together without the instructions.

Working Memory – the ability to hold information in your head and to be able to concentrate on a task – e.g., remembering telephone numbers or being able to do mental arithmetic without having to write down the numbers.

Processing Speed – how quickly you can understand and react to visual information – e.g., when reading pages of text.

Brain Profiles – Flat vs Spiky

If we were to look at the general population, the scores for each of the tests would fall around the average mark (90-109). Often people see *average* as not a particularly good thing, but this is not fair. Average means that a person is *competent and able* in that particular area. It places the person squarely in the majority of the population.

The following chart shows a neuro-typical person; someone who is not dyslexic or dyspraxic, for example. Typically, you tend to see a flatter profile across the four different areas which means scores tend to be close together. Of course, everyone has strengths and weaknesses, so the profile may not be completely flat, but you don't get the wide spread of scores as is commonly seen with the dyslexic profile.

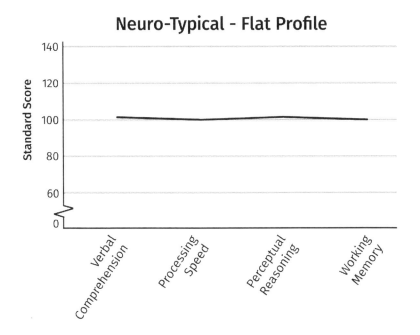

Neuro-Typical - Flat Profile

The next chart shows someone with neurodiversity – e.g., dyslexia. With these people, you tend to see wider spikes, which may mean significant weaknesses in some areas, but also defining strengths in others.

A typical dyslexic profile can show strengths in verbal comprehension and perceptual reasoning, but weaknesses in working memory and processing speed. This is just an example, and every person is different, but this *can* be typical of a lot of the clients I see.

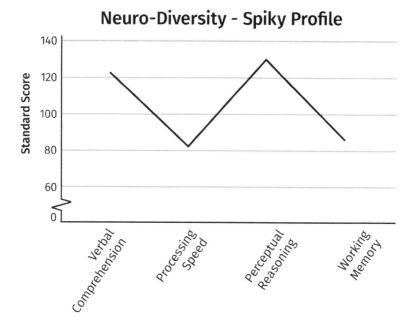

Neuro-Diversity - Spiky Profile

Although these tests give a good indication of abilities and are a good indicator of future performance, **they do not and cannot determine curiosity, motivation, working preferences and achievement** in academia or at work. The great news is there are many strategies that can be employed to compensate for weaknesses in particular areas and these will be covered in later chapters.

The next chapter will look at each of the four areas in more depth.

Typical Uses of Each Cognitive Ability

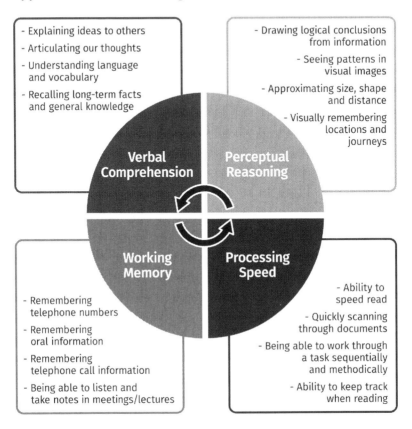

- Explaining ideas to others
- Articulating our thoughts
- Understanding language and vocabulary
- Recalling long-term facts and general knowledge

- Drawing logical conclusions from information
- Seeing patterns in visual images
- Approximating size, shape and distance
- Visually remembering locations and journeys

Verbal Comprehension

Perceptual Reasoning

Working Memory

Processing Speed

- Remembering telephone numbers
- Remembering oral information
- Remembering telephone call information
- Being able to listen and take notes in meetings/lectures

- Ability to speed read
- Quickly scanning through documents
- Being able to work through a task sequentially and methodically
- Ability to keep track when reading

What does this mean? Let's think about where we use some of those skills in real life.

Typical Client Comments

Now that you have a better understanding of cognitive abilities, let's revisit the client comments from the beginning of this book. Here you can see the potential reasons for these strengths and weaknesses.

'I can remember journeys I went on when I was 7 years old (perceptual reasoning) *but I can't remember a phone call I took 3 minutes ago* (working memory)*.'*

'Once I've learnt the information, I can talk about the job until the proverbial cows come home (verbal comprehension) *but I find it really hard to initially process the training guides and it takes me days to read something that would take my colleagues a few hours* (processing speed)*!'*

'My boss doesn't believe that I'm dyslexic because I can spell really well. But she doesn't understand why I can't organise myself.' (Organisation places a heavy load on working memory *as it is cognitively challenging to concentrate on all the different things that are going on in most open-plan offices these days!)*

'I can have a 5-minute conversation with my boss and know exactly what I am expected to do (verbal comprehension) *and even have ideas of how I might approach it, but by the time I walk 2 minutes back to my desk it has completely gone* (working memory)*.'*

'When I learn something new, I am often one of the first people to understand the idea and can talk about it with my peers (verbal comprehension), *but when I have to write it down I can't seem to get the ideas out of my head or structure it* (working memory) *and when I eventually do, it takes me so much longer than others* (processing speed)*.'*

N.B. A lot of people with dyslexia work very hard on the obvious signs of the difficulty such as spelling and writing skills and therefore are assumed to not have dyslexia.

Cognitive Abilities Reflector

Task: Let the journey continue! What else can you learn about 'unique you'?

What would you say about your strengths and weaknesses are in these four areas?

Verbal Comprehension – *Understanding and processing language and the ability to use language to express our thoughts.*

Strengths

Weaknesses

Perceptual Reasoning – *Ability to solve problems visually or use spatial information to make decisions, like finding your way around a new building.*

Strengths

Weaknesses

Working Memory – *Ability to hold information to be able to concentrate on a task.*

Strengths

Weaknesses

Processing Speed – *How quickly a person can understand and react to visual information.*

Strengths

Weaknesses

My Dyslexia – Real Life Case Study A

Name: John
Role: Police Officer
Years in Role: 23

One of my most fascinating cases is the story of John. I think you will agree that this is not only a great example of what can go wrong in the workplace (when people don't understand dyslexia) but also what can be so great about understanding it.

John was referred to me for a work-based needs assessment. He was assessed by another psychologist the year before. He had continued to have difficulties relating to his dyslexia despite his employer making several adjustments to his day-to-day role. I was very keen to understand what had happened to date.

As soon as I met John, I could instantly see he was really struggling to cope with all of the changes that had been made in his job, especially after he was moved to a new role after his diagnostic assessment; a move which his managers considered a useful adjustment. John proceeded to tell me that when he was assessed for dyslexia, he hadn't received much feedback and was simply told that he was dyslexic and a report would follow. This is a personal bugbear of mine, because the best parts of this work (for me personally) are going through the feedback one on one with the client, helping them understand their strengths and weaknesses, and really supporting them in uncovering their full potential.

Not understanding his diagnosis fully, John went back to his employer to discuss what had happened. Despite John being in his role for 23 years, his boss (who assumed it would be helpful) immediately suggested removing him from his role as a police officer and placing him into a role as a call handler taking 999 calls. John was clearly upset about this, but he decided that it might be a good option in the short-term at least.

After John also had difficulties in this role, I was asked to work with him to find a way forward. On meeting John, he gave me a copy of his previous diagnostic assessment which detailed the following scores:

Verbal Comprehension – 95th percentile (superior range)

Perceptual Comprehension – 99th percentile (very superior range)

Working Memory – 5th percentile (much below average range)

Processing Speed – 4th percentile (much below average range)

Don't worry if you do not immediately understand the language but put simply, percentiles just mean how much higher you rank *above* people of your own age group. In this case, John was:

- Above 94% of his peers on the verbal comprehension tests

- Above 98% on the perceptual reasoning tests

In short, he was quite a genius in these areas ranking at the **superior** and **very superior** ranges respectively. Conversely, his working memory and processing speed scores were much lower. When I commented on how remarkable John's top scores were, he immediately said, 'Are they? I didn't understand that previously.'

What became immediately obvious was:

- John should be moved back into his role as a police officer as **his verbal comprehension** abilities were an excellent skill for liaising with teams and speaking to the public.

- John's perceptual reasoning abilities meant that he had highly attuned mental maps of all the places he worked and could visualise every part of them as if he was watching a screen. Indeed, he commented that his colleagues would often call him to ask about alleys, pathways and avenues into which offenders may have run. He could, on cue, visualise these and tell his colleagues over the phone where to focus their search – genius!

- John's weaker working memory was undoubtedly the reason he had found note-taking very difficult whilst under pressure as a police officer and more recently, why he'd found taking 999 calls very difficult. The speed at which these calls had to be completed also made it very stressful, which in turn reduces working memory capacity even more. John had been struggling with processing the information and remembering all the details at speed. He had started to write everything down on paper (long-hand) because he couldn't think, process and type fast enough. He would then try to type the information very quickly after the call.

After he struggled with this method, he formed some very negative assumptions about his overall ability to perform in this or any role.

We promptly got John out of the call centre and back to his police officer role with some minor adjustments, technology and coaching. I am very pleased to report that John has a renewed sense of how his strengths were actually a huge asset to the organisation. This story still makes me emotional to recall, because I remember the man I met at that first meeting and just how quickly things changed for him thereafter with just a little thought and personal attention.

It doesn't matter that John had weaknesses. What matters is how he understood them and therefore how he reduced their impact on his job performance, and ultimately his life. Most importantly, John was able to turn the balance and spend time utilising his strengths instead of struggling with his weaknesses.

With awareness, everything can be worked around.

Chapter 3

Assessment of Neurodiversity

'Without self-awareness we are as babies in the cradle.'

– Virginia Woolf

In this chapter, I am going to explain a little more about the assessment of dyslexia and neurodiversity. Anyone can be assessed for neurodiversity, and I highly recommend it. The assessment is a great opportunity for you fully understand and appreciate your strengths and weaknesses, and it often provides that 'lightbulb moment' when you identify the areas that you find easy and the areas you find more difficult.

A diagnostic assessment is required to find out whether you have dyslexia or dyspraxia and will also help to identify where your strengths and weaknesses lie within those. Understanding how it affects you is the is the first step to managing it.

Assessment Process

The assessment process typically includes:

- **Pre-assessment Questionnaire or Discussion** – to gain a detailed understanding of your background including your strengths, weaknesses and medical and educational history.

- **Cognitive Abilities Assessment** – to gain an overview of your abilities such as: working memory, verbal comprehension, perceptual reasoning and processing abilities.

- **Reading, Writing and Spelling Assessments** – to assess your literacy attainment and identify potential areas of difficulty. Tests include reading, writing, phonemic decoding, writing speed, reading speed.

- **Dyspraxia** – additional motor coordination and visual perception tests are required.

- **Dyscalculia** – Additional tests of mathematics and numerical reasoning are required.

- **ADHD** – Additional screening questionnaires and in-depth background analysis of childhood and education.

This chapter will explore more about cognitive ability assessments, what they are and what they entail. The Wechsler Adult Intelligence Scale (WAIS), currently in its fourth edition, is a battery of tests designed to measure cognitive ability in adults (above the age of 16 years). The WAIS is composed of 10 core subtests, which make up four grouped scores.

The scores from these tests are *standardised* (in order to provide normed groups against which individual scores can be compared) and provide the assessor with a full cognitive profile. This profile allows the assessor to construct a picture of an individual's overall strengths and weaknesses in terms of performance.

The categories and tests used to measure these are:

Verbal Comprehension

Meaning: *Understanding and processing language and the ability to use language to express your thoughts.*

Tests: *Similarities, Vocabulary and Information.*

The tests which measure verbal comprehension focus on the ability to explain and describe ideas and concepts in addition to understanding your crystallised intelligence (i.e., facts/knowledge you have acquired through your experiences). This is typically an area of strength for dyslexic individuals. It can be demonstrated in their ability to express new ideas or explain difficult concepts to peers.

High scorers – People who score highly in this area are likely to do well in settings where they can use their verbal skills such as meetings, discussions and presentations. They are able to ask the right questions and are able to articulate their point. This may also improve communication with their peers and therefore aid successful relationships.

Low scorers – People who score lower here might have difficulty explaining their thoughts, following instructions and understanding complex discussions.

Research – Advantages of High Verbal Abilities

Logan (2009) found that not only do dyslexic people set up more businesses than non-dyslexic individuals, but that **entrepreneurs who had dyslexia were able to grow their companies more quickly than non-dyslexic entrepreneurs**. This can be attributed to interpersonal and communication skills. A study by Logan and Martin (2012) found that **dyslexic entrepreneurs are able to clearly communicate ideas,**

have excellent interpersonal skills and can easily express enthusiasm. These skills enable them to network with people and explain their visions and objectives. It makes them excellent at selling their business ideas. All of this can contribute to their unparalleled success. Successful entrepreneurs with dyslexia include: Sir Richard Branson, Theo Paphitis, Steve Jobs and Bill Gates. Although individuals with dyslexia do have weaknesses, which may cause them to struggle in certain professional environments, or with particular tasks, it certainly does not mean that they cannot achieve as much, if not more than their non-dyslexic counterparts. The most important thing to note is that skills such as strong verbal abilities can provide a strong edge in the business world.

Perceptual Reasoning

Meaning: *Ability to use non-verbal reasoning to apply abstract logic to solve problems.*

Tests: *Block Design, Matrix Reasoning and Visual Puzzles.*

The tests which measure non-verbal reasoning focus on the ability to assess complex relationships and patterns. These are often referred to as tests of *fluid intelligence.*

High scorers – People who score highly in this area tend to have good visual skills and are able to quickly spot patterns in images. Their ability to make connections and link ideas means that they tend to have good lateral thinking and problem-solving skills and may enjoy 'bigger picture' thinking.

Low scorers – People who achieve low scores in this area may have difficulty with visualising information and may take time learning new tasks or processes. They also may not enjoy new and unexpected tasks.

Research – Advantages of Bigger Picture Thinking

In 2001, the University of Bristol reported that one in five UK entrepreneurs were dyslexic. This is double the incidence of dyslexia in the general UK population. In 2009, Professor Logan reported that 35% of entrepreneurs in the USA were dyslexic. That is more than double the general population rate of 15% (Logan, 2012).

This may be attributed to differences in the brain which allow for more 'thinking outside of the box'. Dyslexics may have heightened development of their parvocellular systems, which underlie their holistic, artistic, seeing the 'whole picture' and entrepreneurial talents (Stein, 2001).

'I discovered I could do things better than other people. If I had an idea, I could visualise it in my brain and spin it around. Not everyone can do that. Dyslexia has always been a massive positive for me.'

– Tom Pellereau,
Entrepreneur and winner of the BBC's 'The Apprentice', 2011

Working Memory

Meaning: *Ability to store information to be able to concentrate on a task.*

Tests: *Digit Span and Arithmetic.*

The tests which measure working memory focus on the ability to temporarily hold information and use it to perform a task. For example, remembering all of the information when given directions or performing mental arithmetic. Working memory is akin to concentration or attention.

High scorers – People who score highly here will find it easy to remember directions, phone messages and instructions and would find it easy to transfer information from one source to another (e.g. copying long numbers to a different page or screen).

Low scorers – Those who score lower on this set of tests may also struggle with remembering verbal information – for example, when taking phone messages.

N.B. Working memory and short-term memory are often used interchangeably but they are very different systems. Working memory refers to processing and storage of information. Short-term memory is concerned with just storage.

Research – The Brain and Working Memory

Typically, people with dyslexia tend to have a weaker working memory than non-dyslexics, therefore they are more likely to make mistakes when recalling verbal information.

Researchers show that the reason for this is that, when tested, dyslexics often show lower activation in the working memory areas (namely, the left superior parietal lobule and the right inferior prefrontal gyrus) when the memory load is increased (Beneventi et al., 2010).

Dyslexic individuals are usually competent at recalling information forwards on the digit span test. However, they struggle with recalling the numbers when they are presented backwards. This is consistent with the results of a study conducted by Vasic et al. (2008). These researchers found that dyslexic individuals struggle with the manipulation of verbal information, rather than the storage of it. This is particularly true when cognitive (i.e. 'thinking') demands are high.

Processing Speed

Meaning: *How quickly a person can understand and react to visual information.*

Tests: *Symbol Search and Coding.*

Processing speed refers to our ability to focus attention, visually scan and react to information quickly and accurately. Processing speed requires motor coordination and an ability to work quickly.

High scorers – People who score highly will be able to process information quickly and are likely to be able to read and write quickly. Data entry and completing spreadsheets may feel easy for these people.

Low scorers – People with lower processing speed scores might find dealing with forms, spreadsheets and data entry more difficult than their peers. They may work slower than their peers and can therefore become frustrated with not being able to complete the same volume of work, despite being very skilled in other areas of their work.

Research – The Brain and Processing Speed

Shaul and Breznitz (2007) found evidence to explain why dyslexic individuals generally present with a slower processing speed. They conducted a study which measured the rate at which visual information was transferred from the right to the left hemisphere so that it can then be used in a writing task. Their results showed that in dyslexics, the information was transferred across the corpus callosum 5-6 milliseconds slower than in the non-dyslexic participants. This suggests it is the delay in transferring the data across the brain that causes a slower overall processing speed, rather than the initial 'seeing' of the information.

Assessment of Attainments – Literacy

Literacy attainments are also measured as part of the dyslexic/dyspraxic assessment. These primarily focus on:

Spelling
The ability to spell a number of age-related words correctly.

Word Reading
Reading a list of age-related single words.

Reading Comprehension
Reading passages to assess understanding by answering a number of questions pertaining to the piece(s).

Phonemic Decoding
Understanding the sounds within words. This is measured by asking the client to read a number of 'made-up' words or jumbled phrases to test the ability to isolate phonemes.

Reading Speed

The time taken to read a set of passages.

Writing Speed

A word-per-minute score is obtained from copying a standard sentence.

Free Writing

A timed writing test to assess an individual's ability to articulate and structure his or her ideas or responses related to a set question.

This list is typical of the assessment process but is not exhaustive. The psychologist should assess the individual assessments needed for each client.

My Dyslexia – Real Life Case Study B

 Name: Jonathan K
Profession: Entrepreneur
Years in Role: 20

When did you realise you thought differently?

Good question. At school, when studying, no matter how many times I tried, there were some subjects I just could not get my head around and my marks were very rarely good. For other students, these same activities seemed like no big deal, so I just thought I was stupid.

At work, I would look at a problem and see a solution which to me was perfectly obvious and logical and the most effective way of achieving what needed to be done. I just assumed it was so obvious that everyone else could see it. After many years, it finally dawned on me that what I thought was obvious to me was not necessarily obvious to anyone else and this had to be pointed out to me. Only then did the message finally sink in.

What are your strengths?

I would say my core strengths are:

Ability to get on with others – I am very good at meeting people or at introducing myself to strangers and very quickly putting them at ease and entering into a good conversation.

Planning capabilities – which were developed to get things done.

Creativity – I have ideas all the time, but I do sometimes need to pass them by people to double check that they are reasonable and worth doing. Sometimes I do not discuss what I have thought of, because I just know it is the right thing to do.

What are your weaknesses?

Forgetful – my short-term memory is not great. I can forget anything and everything within seconds, whether it is keys to let myself back into my home, money to go shopping with, people's names, items I have just bought (and it is not uncommon to leave my credit card in the reader for the item I have just bought!)

Distractions – I get distracted very easily and it is usually me distracting myself with new ideas/thoughts and then starting a different project without completing the one I should be doing!

Routine paperwork – I almost go into a mini depression at the prospect of any routine paperwork (it can be as simple as writing an invoice). I will put it off for days/weeks, even though it is often to my immediate advantage to do it.

What are the best things about being dyslexic/neuro-diverse?

For me, the benefits have increased as life has progressed.

Who I am attracted to – once I started working, I was intuitively drawn to people who were entrepreneurial in their outlook and who had a different approach to work and the way of achieving things. Often, I can tell if someone is dyslexic from the way they do things and from what they say. If it is the case, there is that immediate connection, which is great.

The ability to get on with people – I find it very easy to chat with people from all sorts of backgrounds. I have always preferred face-to-face talking and my ability to engage with people anywhere (whether it be a stranger in a coffee shop or someone I have just been introduced to) is very strong. It just comes naturally.

Creativity – for me this is the number one strength. I just know the ideas will come and that I can rely on my excellent problem-solving skills. I have ideas all the time, but I must be careful not to be distracted, which is too easy to do! The other thing is that sometimes my ideas seem perfectly natural and the feedback I get is that what I have suggested is really something to be proud of.

What are your top 3 strategies that help you work better? Anything at all! These can be practical, models, psychological.
Poor short-term memory – mine is appalling and something I need to find alternative solutions to. I constantly lose things, so I have routines where I leave my wallet, phone and keys in the same place at home and I always carry them in the same pockets, regardless of what I wear (if the clothes have pockets!). Another strategy I use is that whenever I get up to leave somewhere (whether a restaurant, a train, a shop counter, etc....), I stop, turn around and for 2 to 3 seconds purposefully check that I have everything.

Distractions – I can and do get distracted in about a millisecond on a regular basis. I find the discipline of doing a weekly plan at the weekend for the forthcoming week, and then a daily plan each day first thing in the morning helps me to stay focused and means that I get a lot done. So, by the end of the week, I feel really satisfied, which is fantastic!

Routine paperwork – any paperwork can be a real struggle for me. So, for work that needs to be done on a regular basis, such as tax returns, I allocate time in my diary for doing it, well ahead of the completion date, and treat it as I would an important meeting. I then have a pre-determined reward for completing the task, which could be an evening out to see a film/go to my favourite restaurant or just a simple drink/food, which is something I do not usually have, but a bit of an indulgence! In addition to the satisfaction of doing the task, I also get the satisfaction of getting it in early.

Chapter 4

Disclosure – Should You Tell Your Employer?

'The greatest prison people live in is the fear of what people think.'

– Anonymous

Do I disclose or not disclose?

My answer to this question is always the same. I think ultimately it is a personal choice, but the chances are it will become evident at some point, so you may as well raise it with your employer early on. Not because it's *dyslexia* per se, but because we ALL have strengths and weaknesses, and those are generally highlighted quite quickly in any role. So why put yourself under the stress of wondering how or when yours might be 'discovered'?

I know it is a real concern, and people are genuinely worried about being discriminated against or being treated unfairly. Therefore, I think the answer lies in *how* you raise the issue. What I tend to notice is that people do themselves a disservice by just stating 'I have dyslexia', because they are so much more than the *difficulties associated* with dyslexia! The same statement also tends to be stressful for the manager or recruiter, because they may not know anything about it other than popular and limiting misconceptions.

Selling Your Strengths

I always tell clients to consider your 'pitch'. For example:

'I have dyslexia. What this means is that I have above average verbal and reasoning skills (as mentioned in my assessment). This means I'm very good with relating complex ideas to customers and solving problems, especially in strategic issues.

What this also means is that I sometimes have difficulty with (insert your areas of weakness here, e.g. processing or short-term retention) and so I may have to write things down sometimes and use my own strategies like mind-mapping so I don't forget.'

The above is just an example, but you can see it's a very different message to 'I have dyslexia', which is often said tentatively and apologetically. It shouldn't be! It is also important to not be shy about saying where your strengths are. I know this is difficult for all of us, whether dyslexic or not. For those with dyslexia, it makes a big difference to clearly know what your strengths are and to be able to easily describe them to someone else when needed. Managers and colleagues want to know where your strengths are so they can utilise you to the fullest. This is very important to remember.

I always encourage clients to consider the other person's point of view, and to be understanding of the fact that they may not know anything about neurodiversity either. They may really want to help but have no idea what to do or say. In my experience, the lack of *understanding* is the issue, not a *lack of motivation* to support.

I would suggest you do disclose but ensure that you have your unique pitch – and one which tells your story. The point here is about *enabling not labelling.*

Reflector – Developing Your Personal Pitch

Task: Time to let others know your strengths and challenges!

Complete the following statements and then turn them into a paragraph which you can easily relay to your manager, employer or colleagues. It is much easier to have a fully prepared statement to recall, than to try and think about it in the moment. It will also allow you to focus on your strengths, and therefore make you feel more confident about sharing the information. Saying this out loud is as important to you as well as the listener so you can really internalise your skills.

Complete the following:

I have (dyslexia/dyspraxia/neurodiversity). This means I will perform exceptionally well in creative/people focused roles (delete as appropriate) and be able to make a real difference to the organisation. For example, I have strengths in:
(Examples – verbal abilities, problem-solving, presentations, teamwork.)

1) Put your top ability first.

2)

3)

This also means that I have sometimes had difficulties with:
(Examples – structuring documents, completing work quickly, organising my workload. Only list two here so the positives outweigh the weaknesses.)

1)

2)

I sometimes use the following to support me:
(I would start with the positive such as the strategies used to get things done, and again give an example of how this adds value to the workplace; e.g. prioritisation strategies – which means I am very good at forward planning. Examples – specialist software, dictaphone, headphones, prioritisation strategies, discussions with colleagues.)

1)

2)

3)

Legal Considerations

The Equality Act 2010 legally protects people from discrimination in the workplace, and in many aspects of wider society. It replaced and simplified 116 separate pieces of equality-related legislation; combining them into one act including the Disability Discrimination Act (1995).

The Equality Act defines and protects the right of disabled people. It places duties on those who provide services, education and employment, and it encourages employers and employees to work together to break away from rigid employment practices and to find flexible ways of working that may benefit the whole workforce. Under the Equality Act, employers have a duty to ensure that their policies, practices and procedures in areas of staff recruitment and retention are non-discriminatory. This includes terms of employment offered, opportunities for promotion, transfers, training, or receiving any other employment-related benefit.

The Equality Act's definition of a disabled person is as having *'a physical or mental impairment which has a substantial and long-term adverse effect on their ability to carry out normal day-to-day activities.'*

Reasonable Adjustments

Examples of adjustments the employer may consider include:

- providing specialised or adapted equipment

- making instructions and manuals more accessible

- providing a reader/scribe

- being flexible about working hours and allowing different start and finish times to help with concentration

- making adjustments to the work environment

- allocating some of the work to someone else or redesigning job descriptions

- providing coaching or retraining if an employee cannot do their current job any longer

- transferring an individual to another post or place of work

You have the right to access these kinds of interventions. You may want to do this through the Access to Work scheme (a government-run scheme that provides funding and advice for any specific interventions recommended through the 'needs assessment' process).

Chapter 5

Wider Strengths
Personality Profiling and Neurodiversity (The Isaacs Technique)

'I can only be me. Everyone else is taken.'

– Oscar Wilde

So far, we've analysed your cognitive abilities and got you thinking about your strengths and weaknesses, but what about personal preferences and individual differences? These are areas of psychology that often are not considered when testing individuals, but these areas are, I think, hugely important. This is why I have developed the 'Isaacs Technique of Understanding Strengths' (I.T.U.S.) which looks at cognitive abilities, attainments *and* the wider strengths in personality preferences (the Big Five).

The Big Five Personality Traits are the core characteristics that we all have. These have been verified by several independent researchers since the 1960s.

Big Five Overview

	Low Scorers	**High Scorers**
Openness to Experience	Conventional	Creative
Conscientiousness	Relaxed approach to deadlines	Imaginative
Extroversion	Quiet Reserved	Energy from others. Gregarious
Agreeableness	Happy to challenge Highly assertive	Aims to reduce conflict Highly collaborative
Proneness to Worry	Calm Even-tempered	Worried Emotional

We all fall along a continuum of each of these scales. How we live, work and relate to others will be heavily influenced by our personality profile. That is not to say we don't use all of these traits at different times in our life – but we tend to have a preference for what feels more comfortable to us. Take me as an example. I fall naturally towards the higher end of Openness to Experience and Agreeableness. If you ask me to be involved in a project I will ask you, 'What's the vision? How are we going to do it? How can we make it interesting and fun? What's the point?' All of these questions relate directly to openness to experience. I will also ask, 'Who is going to be involved? How do they feel about it?' These all relate to the Agreeableness scale. Trying things in a new way and thinking outside of the box will be at the top of my agenda, as will working with others and developing strong relationships.

Someone at the lower end of Agreeableness, however, may be thinking more about the results or the 'end point' and how they can delegate resources and get it done, rather than having the people focus. A high Conscientiousness scorer may focus on timeframes, detail, schedules and certainty. They will want to know what they specifically have to do, the outputs and when it has to be completed by.

My experience is that people with neurodiversity will have a profile just as varied as everyone else's. This is important, as it raises some very important questions such as: How do your cognitive abilities affect your preferences and is it also possible for your preferences to affect your cognitive abilities? The work on neuroplasticity discussed in Chapter 1 would certainly agree with this latter hypothesis. For example, if you have a weaker working memory, are you likely to avoid tasks where you have to hold a lot of information in your head, and prefer tasks where you can instead use your bigger picture, visual abilities? Would that, in turn, affect your personality profile and mean you gravitate towards bigger picture thinking/strategic type tasks?

It would exceed the scope of this book to attempt to fully explore and answer this question (maybe that could be my next book!), but it is an important question we should consider alongside cognitive ability testing.

The I.T.U.S. technique which encompasses both factors has had very positive feedback from clients because it allows them to think about their preferences from a wider angle. Understanding yourself on many levels is incredibly useful for understanding your strengths and weaknesses and therefore devising effective strategies for top performance.

N.B – The above technique is not compulsory for a diagnostic assessment and is only recommended as a way of understanding your personal profile on a deeper level.

Personality Reflector

Spend a few minutes considering where you sit on these measures. Just consider what you prefer. For example, if someone asked you to work on a large project with them:

1) What would be the first thing that would go through your head?

2) What would be your concerns?

3) What would you perceive as challenges?

4) What would you be most excited about?

From these answers, consider where you might sit on each of the Big Five and devise your own 'mini-profile' to use for questions 5 and 6.

5) What are the top three strengths of your preference?

6) How can I use my style more in my work?

7) What do I need to do in my work to ensure that my challenges are minimised?

Compare This to a Colleague's Approach!

It may be useful to complete this exercise from your own and also from a colleague's perspective to think about how they might approach the task differently. Ask yourself:

- What are the challenges with these different approaches when working together?

- How might I overcome them from the outset?

Multiple Intelligences – Intelligence Comes in All Shapes and Sizes

Now you understand how cognitive abilities and personality factors affect you, let's start devising *your key* strengths.

Before we do, it is useful to remember that the types of intelligence mentioned so far are just the ones used in the assessment of neurodiversity, including dyslexia, dyscalculia and dyspraxia. Gardner (1993) suggested that there are actually seven multiple types of intelligence. These are:

1. **Linguistic** Reading, writing, talking or poetry

2. **Logical/Mathematical** Ability with numbers or analysis

3. **Spatial** Navigating, driving or architecture

4. **Musical** Playing an instrument, singing, writing/composing music

5. **Bodily-kinaesthetic** Sports/dance ability

6. **Interpersonal** Ability to understand others

7. **Intrapersonal** Level of own self-awareness

Wider Strengths Reflector

Intelligence Area	Score 1-10	Seen in My Ability To...
Linguistic Reading, writing, talking		
Logical Ability with numbers		
Spatial Navigating/orientation		
Musical Playing/singing/composing		
Bodily-kinaesthetic Sports/dance ability		
Interpersonal Understanding others		
Intrapersonal Self-awareness		

Example Completed Form – Cheryl Isaacs

Intelligence Area	Score 1-10	Seen in My Ability To...
Linguistic Reading, writing, talking	8	Present training courses and conferences
Logical Ability with numbers	8	Quick arithmetic ability
Spatial Navigating/orientation	3	Getting lost easily and forgetting major landmarks
Musical Playing/singing/ composing	4	I don't have a lot of ability here but plenty of enthusiasm which has allowed me to learn the drums (badly!)
Bodily-kinaesthetic Sports/dance ability	4	I have rhythm but can easily forget dance moves so wouldn't consider this a key strength
Interpersonal Understanding others	9	I have had considerable feedback on my ability here in my work as a psychologist so am confident that I can relate to people easily
Intrapersonal Self-awareness	8	I consider myself quite able here as I have had to undergo a great deal of work in this area. I definitely do not consider myself to be the finished article, however

You might want to consider these, then add them to your personal pitch as discussed in Chapter 4 under Disclosure.

As discussed previously, research conducted with the growth mindset has demonstrated that skills can be developed with the right mindset, so your strengths may not be set but waiting to be discovered!

IQ and Personality Tests Only Measure What Can Be Measured!

Moreover, we must not forget skills that cannot be measured such as humour, artistic flair and creativity. Do you have any of these that you would add to your list of strengths?

Furthermore, Sternberg (1984) suggested that intelligence is just applying what you already know to new contexts – you just need to break down the underlying processes and understand how they transfer. For example, if you are very methodical and enjoy completing tasks in a logical sequence, you might also enjoy projecting management. If you enjoy explaining ideas to others, you might also enjoy training.

Spend some time considering how the strengths you have are transferable and complete the table on the following page.

Transferable Skills Reflector

Have a go at completing the following table to highlight how you can use your skills in different contexts.

Strength	Where Might this Skill Be Transferable?
E.g. Interpersonal skills	Working with stakeholders/clients on new projects

My Dyslexia – Real Life Case Study C

Name: Robin
Profession: Strategic Officer
Years in Role: 20

When did you realise you thought differently?
Almost as far back as I can remember, I can recall teachers pointing out 'silly and inconsistent' mistakes I had made. I have always been aware that my memory is not consistent and that my mental agility and ability to recall facts quickly can be poor. For example, I have vivid memories of reading extensively around topics before seminars at university (but remembering very little!) and then sitting in the seminar wondering where the ideas and comments others were making came from, when I knew that in reality most of them hadn't done much background reading.

At work, I heard comments about my work being of 'variable quality' or work that was 'let down' by simple mistakes or work that was 'below reasonable expectations of someone in my position' or that I had 'caused too much work for others'. These were legion, but more importantly, accurate. This hurt more, because in my heart of hearts I knew that despite huge amounts of effort on my part and a really genuine wish to work more effectively, the comments were true. I just couldn't see a way around them. To add to the frustration, I have also always known there are things I can do easily compared to others.

I have therefore always been aware of my shortcomings but also frustrated (and embarrassed) because the mistakes that I made on paper didn't concur with my brain – nor did they match my expectations of what I can do or the image I have of myself.

At that point, towards the middle of my career, I had also begun to justify my shortcomings with thoughts like: 'It's just personality conflict; I don't have the problem' and 'In the big picture, are such small mistakes really that important?' I would say, 'It's just my ageing brain' (can't deny that one!) and 'Maybe I should just accept my lot' or 'Perhaps I am in too senior a position'. I took comfort with things like, 'I have a lovely family, so why should I let work bother me?'

What are your strengths?

- Verbally very dextrous – exceptionally high verbal comprehension abilities
- Writing – when I have space and time, I can craft very fluent text – for example, when writing speeches
- Empathy with others – comfortable having conversations with anyone at any level, and sensitive to the issues they face
- Ability to get on with people at any level and create excellent working relationships
- Stakeholder management
- IT – particularly supporting others to use IT
- Extremely patient
- Confident speaking publicly – as long as I have a script and time to prepare!

What are your weaknesses?

It is sometimes easiest to show you what others see. Here is an extract from my line manager in a letter to occupational health asking for me to be referred, which sums up my weaknesses:

'Inconsistent performance can range from good to not performing at a satisfactory level in what might be termed the 'basics'. His work

often contains a number of mistakes that are not corrected even when they have been pointed out. He often fails to do everything that is asked of him on a task.'

I believe this relates to my below average working memory.

I have found the following areas on occasion challenging:

- Concentrating on one task – prioritising or working efficiently
- Note-taking
- Multitasking
- Attention to detail / concentration
- Time management –completing tasks within a set time and sequencing of information
- Abstract problem-solving (ability to analyse information, detect patterns
- and relationships and solve problems on a complex, intangible level)
- Spatial perception (ability to perceive and visually understand outside spatial information such as features, properties, measurement, shapes, position and motion)
- Ability to perceive visual details
- Learning and storing new information (e.g. remembering oral instructions)
- Recalling and using information at a later date

What are the best things about being dyslexic/neuro-diverse?

Until my assessment a few years ago, I can't really say that I was aware that I 'thought differently', but I did have the feeling that with 20 years of my career still to run, there was a need to consider how I would manage the future. Previously, I had no concept of the word *neurodiversity*. I am afraid I also held a common misconception that dyslexia was about having challenging issues with reading and writing. I was however, always aware that like anyone, I have strengths and weaknesses in certain areas.

The assessment of having a neuro-diverse, spiky-dyslexic profile gives me, for the first time in my life, a clear sense of direction towards my strengths. It helped me understand how there is more value in considering and pursuing roles that play to my strengths and that I had a set of tools that I can adapt to help manage areas I find more challenging.

What are your top strategies that help you work better?

Mind-map software – particularly production of a weekly dashboard. I add tasks as the week progresses and use colour to show progress in a traffic light system – red (not done), amber (in process), green (completed). I also link brief notes to each task, so I have a summary of progress for each event.

Electronic diary – used as a brought forward file. If I send an email, for example, requesting information, etc., I also diarise a time to chase the email (if necessary). I also attach a copy of the original email to this new event, which saves me having to go back to my sent box and find the original request. I also maintain an A4 paper-based diary which (along with the mind-map weekly dashboard) I find is the best way to maintain a 'helicopter view' of meetings etc.

Managing the inbox – eases multitasking and makes you less easily distracted. This has been borrowed from John Levitt from his personal blog on dyslexia http://www.dyslexicprofessional.com/

Set up just four folders – 'This week', 'Last week', 'Older emails' and 'Actions'

Just have one day's worth of email in the inbox and try to clear that every day. At the end of each day, drag the contents (read or not) to a 'This Week' folder, where it stays until the end of the week. At the end of the week, drag the entire contents of 'This week' to a 'Last Week' folder. When there is an email that requires action, drag to your 'Actions' folder.

This system needs to be regularly reviewed for it to work.

Newsletters – I have also unsubscribed from all newsletters that aren't strictly work focused, so there is less chance to be distracted.

Anything else you would like to say about it?

The assessment gave me affirming clarity, a purpose and a clear direction of travel. I now have a much better understanding of what I can and can't do and therefore what I should and shouldn't do in terms of the rest of my career and in my personal life. For example, the assessment has given me a renewed self-confidence in that I have a document which shows that some of what I have found challenging over my life was not due to a lack of competence or some kind of slapdash/arrogant approach on my part.

I can confidently say the assessment was one of the most useful few hours I have had for a very long time.

Other Useful Tips

Meetups – free events are arranged by dyslexics for dyslexics (particularly in London) and can provide useful tips, advice, contacts and pointers.

Twitter – search on #dyslexia and #neurodiversity for links to organisations and help across the world.

Part 2

Typical Challenges and How to Overcome Them

Chapter 6

Memory

'I swear if my memory was any worse, I could plan my own surprise party!'

– Anonymous

In this chapter and the following chapters, we are going to look at how you can implement some simple strategies that allow you to exercise power and quality control over how you work.

In this chapter, we will look at some effective strategies for memory. In my practice, I see many clients who often report that they have a poor memory. This cannot be strictly true, because **memory isn't one function, but more of a mix of different types of memory, which help us with a range of different functions.**

As we saw earlier in Chapters 2 and 3, people with dyslexia and neurodiversity tend to have a weaker *working memory*, which will affect tasks such as remembering and manipulating information in the moment or short term, but they may also have very strong long-term or visual memory. Clients will often tell me about journeys or places they went to as a child, but they can't clearly remember a conversation from five minutes ago.

In this chapter we are going to cover:

Mindset Strategies
- Automaticity – The Art of Habit Forming

Practical Strategies
- Collection Buckets – Emptying Your Brain
- To-do Lists
- Meeting Notes Made Easy
- Association – Remembering Names
- Utilising Others
- Musical Memory
- Transposing Numbers Strategy
- Chunking and Summarising
- Visual Learning
- Get Deep Before Sleep
- Maintenance Memory Vs Elaborative Memory
- Guess Work Memory
- Spaced Learning
- Whole Body Learning
- Interview Strategies – Telling a Story

Technological Interventions
- Dictaphones
- Mind-mapping
- Phone Reminders
- Maintenance Memory Vs Elaborative Memory

Mindset Strategies

Automaticity – the Art of Habit Forming

Before we begin to think about strategies for typical challenges, I would like to get you thinking about what needs to be in place for these strategies and ideas to work.

Automaticity is the ability to do things without occupying the mind with the low-level details required to do them, allowing it to become an automatic response pattern or *habit*. It is usually the result of learning, repetition and practice. If a skill is not automatised, it will be disrupted by the concurrent processing of a second skill, because two skills are then competing for limited attentional resources.

Automaticity refers to knowing how to perform some arbitrary task at a competent level without requiring conscious effort. In other words, it is a form of unconscious competence. With experience, the way we approach a problem becomes reduced to routine. This automaticity frees up mental resources (attentional capacity or working memory), allowing for effective problem-solving.

When approaching a problem, there is always more that could be processed than we have the mental capacity to handle. Expertise in an area enables our minds to automatically address the problem at a simple level, thus freeing up mental energy. This energy can be re-invested in the problem at a more complex level, fostering lateral thinking and creativity (Bereiter, 2005).

When learning a new skill or approach to something, like attending a training course, for example, always ensure that you have the time to apply these new skills in the workplace, and to re-enforce the new connections in the brain until they become *automatic*.

Creating automaticity in the way you perform this new task allows for greater investment of resources and, as a result, increased productivity and innovative thinking.

One of the best ways to ensure automaticity is to consider your supporting habits.

Habits and Supporting Habits

It is not enough to just try and develop a habit on its own. We all have the experience of saying something like: 'I'm going to start a new diet/workout regime/write that book,' only to find that we try it once or twice, and then find it really hard to keep doing. Basically, it doesn't work because it feels like a mountain to climb, especially when it's a new challenge or series of tasks.

The best thing you can do is consider these questions:

What will make this easier?

What could I do first that will act as a support for my main habit?

For example, I know that if I put my gym clothes on as soon as I walk through the front door (the supporting habit), it will guarantee the later workout, because this supporting habit is not difficult to achieve. In fact, I would have been changing clothes anyway. I now just wear the gym clothes straight away, and I'm already halfway there mentally. It would feel very weak to take them off without even a short workout, so, either way, it's a win! What often happens is that I will think, 'Well I'm not really in the mood, so I'll do a short run,' but of course I end up running longer as I get 'into the zone'.

The same is true of any habit. You need to first give yourself the best form of preparation for that task or activity. The supporting habit is normally quite simple, but it will hugely increase your chances of doing the main one. For example:

New Habit: Dedicating the first ten minutes of your day to goal-setting the top three priorities of that day.

Supporting Habit: Ensuring that your inbox isn't opened until 9:10 every day, so that you have complete focus on your new main habit and can't get distracted. No checking your phone or social media either!

Practical Strategies

Mental Collection Buckets – Emptying Your Brain

Working memory and short-term memory are finite cognitive resources. Information, therefore, needs to be 'emptied' regularly from your brain to ensure that you can concentrate on other important things. Consider what your 'collection buckets' are and ensure they are regularly filled (and emptied, for that matter!) For example, some people like to write everything down in a notebook and some like to mind-map their ideas.

Cognitive Load Theory by Professor John Sweller suggests that our brains will randomly start picking things to remember when overloaded. Of course, this will not typically be the things you wanted to focus on, so it is important not to let it overflow in the first place. For example, if you're feeling stressed, write down all the things you need to do, identify the top three and then work on them in priority. This can be applied to a project, for going on holiday, for organising events or even prioritising building work. I have successfully used this for builders working on my house!

To-do Lists – Daily or Ongoing?

Most people understand the importance of a to-do list in serving their memory. However, it is useful to consider if the one you are using suits you and your personality.

For example, I used to do take the classic approach of re-writing a new to-do list every time I needed to 'empty my brain'. However, not only did writing a new list take more time, but I randomly had the realisation that throwing away the list at the end of each day did not allow me to see all of my lovely achievements down the line!

I therefore bought a new book (or you can do this on your phone) and started keeping an ongoing list and numbered each task. I also highlighted completed tasks in a different colour so it was very easy to distinguish between them. A key driver of behaviour for me is *achievement*, so the only thing I needed to get me motivated in the morning was seeing all the things I had completed over the last few months and I was in my 'flow' state.

This approach achieved three things for me; emptying my brain and freeing up cognitive resources, logging all of my tasks and keeping me organised, plus motivating myself in the process by allowing me to feel good about all the things that I had completed.

Having **one** easy-to-follow system will also help. An easy way of doing this is to add notes on your phone and add important dates and meetings onto your phone calendar which can then be linked up to your main computer. Therefore, you have easy access to everything you need to do, wherever you are. An easy system for this is the software Dropbox, which is free and simple to use. Moreover, when adding to or taking away from the list, you can be sure that the information will be the same across all of your devices.

Supporting Habit: just having a to-do list or a diary is not enough. To make this process useful to plan and organise your workload, it is important to schedule five minutes at the beginning of the day, and five minutes after lunch or at the end of the day to look through your list and make sure you know are reviewing and prioritising regularly.

Meeting Notes Made Easy – Simplicity at Its Best

If you struggle to take messages or to write important information in meetings, or if you end up missing key points in discussions because you are constantly trying to write everything down verbatim, you could benefit from using a note-taking template.

A classic mistake when taking notes is to use a jot pad to write down full sentences or ideas. Not only does this not serve your memory, but it also makes you feel incredibly disorganised when you are later trying to decipher what you have written. A template will make it much easier for you to record key information in meetings/phone calls, without worrying about whether you have forgotten to write the key points. You can then use this simplified, standard information to refer back to later.

I always promote simplicity, and there is no easier strategy than the 'What, When, Who' template. I use this myself in my company team meetings. I have also recommended it to a number of clients who have said that it has transformed their ability to write effective notes and keep track of key actions. They have reported having simpler and more effective notes, which can be referred to easily when checking progress later on. The template looks like this:

What	When	Who

As you can see, this template is very simple. You can adapt it to fit your needs or the particular issues/themes that reoccur in your business or role but generally these three columns will cover most of the information that you will find noteworthy. The template also prevents you having to write full sentences, as it is very clear what they refer to. It is best to use the same template every time so that information retrieval is quick and your working memory is not overloaded by trying to process different styles.

Association – Remembering Names and Details

If you have difficulty remembering people's names, it is useful to look for other traits in people to help you make an association with their name. These traits can be either behavioural or physical. For example, someone who is tall and called Ben could be remembered as 'Big Ben' or someone who talks a lot and is called Charlotte could be remembered as 'Chatty Charlie'. Making the information meaningful to you makes it more memorable, and consequently easier to recall. People with neurodiversity quite often have an incredibly strong visual memory, so this method can be very helpful.

Here are the steps you can take:

1. Listen to the persons' name and repeat, if you can, 'I am pleased to meet you, Fred.' Repetition always helps.

2. As they talk, think about the name and whether it rhymes with anything. If so, can you use that?

3. If not look at them and see if you can make a link between the person, how they look, what they do. For example, for a teacher who teaches French you might think 'French Fred'.

4. Each time you see them, think of the whole catchy name you have for them e.g. 'French Fred'.

Long-term Memory of Names

For long-term storage of names and important information, consider the following technique:

1. Write them down with a description of the person.

2. Put them into logical groupings, such as: Company A, Team A.

3. Put the information in a place you can easily find, such as in a file for that company, project, place, or in your contact details for that company.

Retention of Important Details

Alternatively, if you are required to remember facts or details of an event, doing some research around the topic can help anchor the information and make it meaningful and easier to recall. This method helps you remember information as a story, rather than trying to recall random, independent streams of information. For example, if a new business term or model is presented at an office meeting, spend some time independently researching what that means, and don't simply rely on what you were told in the meeting. This will create an independent association with the new concept and make it easier to remember and recall than merely being told about it (even if you took notes).

In this way, you are taking information presented in other peoples' terms, and converting it into your own language and images. This will impress the concept in your mind in a way that you can effectively identify and recall at a later time.

Mnemonics

Mnemonics can be very effective in helping people to remember specific information. The silliness of the rhymes usually guarantees long-term recall such as for the eight planets:

My Very Excellent Mother Just Served Us Nachos

- Mars
- Venus
- Earth
- Mercury
- Jupiter
- Saturn
- Uranus
- Neptune

For spelling the word 'necessary':

Never Eat Cake Eat Sausage Sandwiches And Remain Young

It's great fun to make up your own!

Utilising Others – Stating Your Needs

If you are struggling to remember what your manager has told you to do, ask him/her to give you written instructions. Specify whether you prefer bullet points or detailed text. This will allow you to revisit the information in your own time and it will save both of you time later on. This can be done more easily than you might think and can be just asking your manager to send you a confirmation email on the subject or assignment.

Musical Memory

A great way to remember sequences of numbers is to sing the digits in groups of three with varying different tones as you sing. For example, for the number 020-89-220-might be broken down in this way:

020 (low tone), 89 (high pitch), 220 (low tone).

You can do this in your head, so don't worry if you work in an open-plan office! You can see how quickly the tune allows you to remember the number and also makes it a lot more fun.

Transposing Numbers and Letters When Copying

Transposing numbers and letters while reading and writing is a classic dyslexic difficulty, and one that can be very frustrating. Clients will often tell me that they may even know that they are mixing up the numbers when copying, but they cannot stop their brain from doing it.

A very simple solution for this is to first use tracing paper or a very thin piece of paper to trace the digits, sequences, or dates first and then simply re-write over information on the intended page. This will leave indentations on the paper which can just be filled in when you lift the tracing paper. This method only takes seconds, and it has a zero-error rate. Genius!

Chunking and Self-Summarising

When trying to remember long chunks of text, you might find it easier if you highlight the key terms and points on the first read, and then re-read the text a second time for comprehension. By pre-screening the key concepts, you will have a more focused approach on the second read, because your brain will start to focus on the key information. You may also want to chunk key information in different colours, according to:

- Key vocabulary
- Key facts/numbers
- Key theories/models

It is also effective to create your own summary of the main points, and then test yourself on these themes rather than on the whole document. You will find that the rest of the detail will follow more easily once you have retained the core points and converted them into a personal summary.

Visual Learning

Given that people with dyslexia and neurodiversity tend to have a very strong visual brain, you can tap into this skill by utilising mind-maps and visuals where possible. Not only are these great for creativity, but they also help to structure ideas and can increase retention of the ideas.

Instead of sitting at your desk or around a table with the rest of your team, trying to spark creativity or solve a pressing issue, why not take advantage of your visual brain? You can do this by using a whiteboard or by covering your wall in flipchart paper and get everyone involved in adding ideas. This allows the entire team to create a shared mental model upon which they can all agree.

This act of engaging and creating interactive imagery enriches meaning and allows you (and your team) to:

- Clarify what you are trying to achieve
- Gain a holistic view and visualise the results
- Fully engage with the project/task
- Create persistent visual hooks, which helps memory

Neuroscience Research – Did You Know?

Neuroscience research has shown that adding visual elements enhances knowledge retention. According to neuroscience research that is referenced in John Medina's book *Brain Rules*, this might be as a result of something called the 'Pictorial Superiority Effect'.

Participants in studies only remember about 10% of the information presented orally when they are tested 72 hours after instruction, but this increased to 65% when an image was added.

You may therefore also want to consider what other visual aids are available to you. For example, if you're learning about the body, have a picture of it in front of you. If you are learning about different countries, have an atlas in front of you.

Get Deep Before Sleep!

Research has shown that retrieval of information is much greater if read just before sleep.

Make a point of reading your summarised notes before bedtime and you are much more likely to embed the memories in your long-term memory, especially if they are in a visual format.

Maintenance Memory Vs Elaborative Memory

Maintenance memory is where you learn something by rote like dialling a phone number and the information is maintained by the simple repetition of it. Elaborative memory is where you expand and build on the concepts and make links/associations with already stored information. These are both effective models for learning new information – however, the latter improves long-term memory store.

You can improve your elaborative memory by discussing ideas, considering counter views/arguments and trying to create case studies.

Guessing to Improve Memory

Research has shown that guessing is an important resource when trying to retain information. A recent study showed that those who guessed were more likely to remember the information the second time they were asked compared to people who did not guess (Yan, Yu, Garcia & Bjork, 2014). This is probably because guessing makes the search for information a more in-depth cognitive process than just staying quiet.

This may also relate to a concept called 'Perceptual and Semantic Priming'. Priming refers to the phenomenon that prior perception of something leads to easier recall of it later. Therefore, you can increase your memory by introducing small pieces of information before learning more extensive pieces later. This will create 'hooks' in your brain and increase recall.

Spaced Learning

Spaced or distributed learning has been shown to be far more effective for retention than in short time frames (Dunlosky, 2005). When learning something new, focus on microlearning and devise short summaries that are revisited regularly rather than cramming large chunks of training into long days.

Whole Body Learning

'People remember 90 percent of what they do, 75 percent of what they see, and 20 percent of what they hear.' (Ellis, 1997, *Becoming A Master Student*, 8th ed.).

Learning actively can involve your whole body. You can stand up and talk aloud as you learn, using your arms, legs, eyes, ears and voice. Getting your body involved puts energy into the study process and makes it less boring.

You may have tried this with speech, but it also works very well with most forms of key concept learning (rather than complex and detailed work).

Remembering Information at Interviews – Telling a Story

A common concern I often hear from clients is the fear of 'blanking' in interviews. Moreover, they also worry that they are not passing selection procedures because their dyslexia is not being taken into account.

First of all, it is important that you tell employers about any challenges you may have with the process so that the employer can make reasonable adjustments for you. In fact, the law requires them to do so.

However, the concern that you might miss opportunities if you reveal or emphasise your dyslexia or neurodiversity in the selection process is an understandable consideration. This is discussed in Chapter 4 above. Clearly this and natural interview jitters can all combine to make you worry about your performance in these pressurised situations.

It is important, therefore, that you consider using some established techniques such as story-telling when responding to interview questions. It is much easier to address questions by responding with a story that has a start, middle and end, than it is to come up with cold facts or spontaneous examples. The easiest way to do this is to prepare a short story with:

1. A start – which sets out the scenario

2. A middle – which describes what happened, what you achieved and how you went about it

3. An end – which summarises what you learned or gained from the experience, or how you adjusted

Remember, there is nothing wrong with having notes in an interview. Interviewers will welcome short, abbreviated notes that allow you to keep on point. The key is to prepare your stories, and then visualise every part of them several times before the interview. This is a simple but very effective strategy. The issue is not often unsuitability for the role but simply the lack of information being provided.

Technological Interventions

Recording Information

Using a dictaphone is a great way to support your working memory. It can be useful to take this into meetings or use when talking to colleagues about important projects. It will allow you to refer back to what was said, and stop you forgetting key points. If you do not have a dictaphone, or don't want a separate system, you can always use your phone. All modern smartphones have an in-built record function. Just make sure you first get permission from whoever you are recording!

Mind-Mapping Software

Mind-mapping software has proved very effective in helping people recall and retain information. Mind-maps are simply visual charts that illustrate concepts and that show the various components or tasks associated with them. Some people prefer mind-mapping software over paper mind-maps, because they can be saved, edited and turned into a linear form with the switch of a button. Programs such as MindView or MindMeister (free version) have been popular with my clients, but there is a range of products on the market now.

Phone Reminders and Notes

Don't forget to use your phone for notes and reminders. I recommend some very simple ways of doing this. The first is to keep note pages for a few key areas of your life, such as:

- Articles to Read
- People to Contact
- Tasks and Errands

- Books or Articles to Read
- Things to Buy

Richard Branson credits his dyslexia for forming one of his signature management techniques: the habit of always taking notes. He writes in his 2014 book, The Virgin Way, that he learned as a child that if he ever wanted a chance at remembering anything, he needed to jot it down. To this day, he says he carries a notebook everywhere. This is a simple and inexpensive habit, which can be very effective.

Neuroscience Research – Why the Brain Likes Imagery!

Mind-maps are effective because the brain likes imagery. After light has entered the human eye, it is streamed to the primary visual cortex. However, this area of the brain only sees simple shapes. The primary cortex then acts as a relay station that re-directs incoming visual information to as many as 30 other parts of the brain.

The three main information processing areas of the brain are the ventral stream, the dorsal stream and the limbic system. These processing centres are what enable us to create meaning and to gain a better understanding of the world.

'More than 50 percent of the cortex, the surface of the brain, is devoted to processing visual information.' (William G. Allyn, Professor of Medical Optics).

Consequently, you have a lot of brain power that is dedicated to taking in and processing imagery, which is why mind-mapping tends to work so effectively.

Memory Reflector

Before we go any further, it's important to consolidate your learning so far and make sure we start to use some of those supporting habits. The great news is that there are so many brilliant techniques to support your working memory, now you just have to turn them into habits!

Take a moment to consider the following strategy chart. Pick the top three strategies that would work for you. There's space to personalise them to your own needs. What can you start doing today?

Mindset Strategies

Habit/Technique	What Do I Need to Do or Try to Get Started?
Automaticity	Practice, practice, practice! It will be worth it and free up your memory for other tasks.

Practical Strategies

Habit/Technique	What Do I Need to Do or Try to Get Started?
Mental Collection Bucket	Download a mind-map app or draw your own. Use a notes system that talks to all of your devices.
Meeting Notes	Simple template: What? When? Who?
Association	Start getting creative to remember names ('Chatty Charlie'). And repeat their name back to them too!
Utilising Others	Ask for written, bullet-pointed instructions. Don't overload your memory!

Musical Memory	Get humming! Sing digits in different keys to remember them more easily.
Transposing	Get out your tracing paper to avoid errors!
Chunking/Self-summarising	Key vocabulary Key facts/numbers Key theories/models
Visual Learning	Get your whiteboard markers out and get creative! Use mind-maps.
Getting Deep	Read your summarised notes before bed.
Maintenance Memory	Elaborate on your learning. Make links, find relationships and embed your learning more deeply!
Guessing	Always encourage your brain to guess and engage.
Spaced Learning	Little and often will help you to retain more.
Whole Body Learning	Let's get physical. Use your body to help you remember.

Technological Interventions

Habit/Technique	What Do I Need to Do or Try to Get Started?
Dictaphone	Start by recording key information in meetings or ideas as you think of them on-the-go.
Mind-mapping	Try downloading one of the mind-mapping products and start by brainstorming an idea, document or essay. You can also try organising all of your tasks and colour code them for priority – e.g. red for urgent, blue for non-urgent.

Phone Reminders	Start using your phone for reminders, all diary appointments and storing data. Apps such as Dropbox (free) can be synced with your computer and allow you to access all of your files, photos and documents from your phone.

Chapter 7

Mastering Concentration

'*The secret to success in any human endeavour is total concentration.*'

– Kurt Vonnegut

Concentration is a common theme when my clients discuss their dyslexia or neurodiversity. It is also an area that most people would benefit from considering, especially because our modern, open-plan workplaces and technological distractions do nothing to help us to stay focused and in a productive flow-state.

This chapter focuses on the top strategies for maintaining focus and concentration that have most helped my clients. These always seem to fall into two distinct categories – physical and mental. We will cover the following areas:

Improving Physical Concentration

- Noise-cancelling Headphones – Music or Silence?
- Desk Positioning
- Alternating Physical Positions

- Working From Home
- Managing Distractions From Others
- Technological Distractions

Enhancing Mental Focus

- Manage Your Energy Not Your Time
- Cognitive Enhancers
- Eating for Concentration
- Create Excitement – Power Hour
- Personal Goals
- Staying Mindful
- Questioning
- Desk Meditation
- Forget Multitasking – It's Cognitively Impossible

Improving Physical Concentration

Noise-Cancelling Headphones

If you find that the open-plan office arrangement easily distracts you, noise-cancelling headphones can be helpful when working on complex or challenging tasks. Alternatively, some people prefer to have their own music playing instead of hearing the office hum-drum. Try both approaches to see what works best for you.

Reducing 360-Degree Distraction

If you are easily distracted by others, ask to be moved to a corner of the room where you can limit the distraction to 180 degrees. This can make a huge difference to your concentration levels. Where possible, try repositioning your chair at your desk or workstation so you are facing away from the rest of the office and reducing the potential distractions.

Alternating Physical Positions
Try to vary the ways you sit and stand whenever possible. This can increase blood flow to the brain. Height-adjustable desks are now commonly available and allow for easy switching of positions.

Working From Home
Working from home can have a significant and positive effect on concentration, and, therefore, productivity. I recently read some interesting research which found:

- 85% of people surveyed felt that allowing staff to work flexibly enhances employee wellbeing (Institute of Leadership and Management).

- Employees working from home experience greater emotional engagement and reported higher job satisfaction (Chartered Institute of Personnel Development).

- Those who work from home have a 13% performance increase and took fewer breaks and sick days (Stanford University).

- Employees who worked from home reported 25% less stress and 80% reported a better work-life balance (Staples Research).

I'm convinced!

Managing Distractions From Others

Standard Statements

Interruptions from colleagues is a common problem experienced by most people. It can have significant negative implications for people who struggle with concentration. Try managing the interruptions by using statements such as: 'I am just completing this task, but I will come and speak to you in five minutes or at lunchtime.'

I'm a fan of good old-fashioned communication. Most people will relate to the problem and will appreciate you making time for them when you are not distracted.

Surgery Time

You may also find it useful to allocate particular times during the day in which you are available to discuss questions and issues that may arise in the office.

At all other times, or when in the middle of an important task, you may want to let colleagues know that unless it is urgent, you are not available and will speak to them when you are finished. Let them know that your objective is to actually have more time for them and to give the issue the attention it deserves.

Traffic Light System

You may find it useful to have a system where red means 'not available' and green means 'I am available to speak'. I had a client use this to such great effect that his colleagues also started using the same system shortly afterwards. The key is to not use red all the time or you will appear very unhelpful!

Wearing headphones is an alternative method.

Technological Distractions

When trying to proactively concentrate, turn off all pings, reminders, notifications and ringtones from your phone or computer. Shut down email, and only have the screen from which you are working visible at any given time. Consider making a commitment to only look at emails twice a day. You will be amazed at the positive effect this has on your focus and concentration levels. Simple, but very effective.

Enhancing Mental Focus

Manage Your Energy Not Your Time – Circadian Rhythms

A common problem I see for many clients, especially my clients with neurodiversity, is how they manage their energy levels. Given that we all work in very high-paced environments, which also cause some difficult cognitive challenges, it amazes me how few people consider adapting their working days to reflect their own physical and cognitive needs. Sometimes the simplest 'tweaks' can have the biggest impact.

Consider my own profile, for example:

Highest energy in the morning – therefore, this is the best time for me to to complex tasks that require creativity and concentration.

Mid-level energy around lunchtime – therefore, this is a good time to talk to colleagues and clients, which will keep me energised rather than pushing me into an early slump.

Lowest energy in the afternoon – at this time I start to get tired and find it hard to concentrate. This time is best suited to routine and simple tasks that I have completed many times over and that don't require a high cognitive load.

This might be the opposite for you. You might find you are least productive in the morning and that your energy levels increase in the afternoon.

Get to know your rhythm and try and maximise your productive hours. Whilst this may not always be possible, it is very useful to work to your own natural rhythms where you can. It can increase your overall daily performance significantly.

Reflector – Circadian Rhythm

Task: Think about when you are the most energised you.

Mornings are my best or worst time for what?

Afternoons are my best or worst time for what?

Late afternoon is my best or worst time for what?

When my energy is flagging I recharge by:

Cognitive Enhancers – Breaks and Exercise

Breaks – A simple way to improve your concentration is to always take regular breaks. This might seem counterintuitive to getting things done – however, research has shown that taking a 10-minute break every 90 minutes helps your mind relax and recover. This prevents you from overloading your brain and it improves your concentration (in turn, making you more productive and effective). I personally don't call them breaks. I call them **cognitive enhancers.**

When studying/learning, these breaks might need to be in shorter time-frames, e.g. 10 minutes for every 50 minutes of study.

Holidays – have even been shown to increase creativity. After a holiday, people were able to come up with a more diverse range of ideas, indicating higher levels of mental flexibility. This means, after returning home from a vacation, workers are more likely to consider different aspects of a problem and avoid reliance on conventional ideas and routine solutions. Travel may actually broaden the mind! (De Bloom, Ritter et al., 2014).

Exercise – Exercise also improves circulation and reduces stress, thereby improving blood flow and oxygen to the brain. The brain is only 2% of our body mass but uses a remarkable 20% of the oxygen we take into our bodies. In this way, the brain actually thrives when you physically exercise. Exercise also increases the volume of white and grey matter in the brain.

Try walking to or from work or take a walk to somewhere further to get your lunch. Even just walking for 30-45 minutes will improve blood and oxygen flow to the brain, aiding neuroplasticity.

Eating for Concentration

A study by Kings College, London in 2009 showed that having a bowl of cereal at breakfast cuts decline in performance throughout the day by half. The researchers also highlighted data showing that a decline in performance throughout the morning, measured by the ability to pay attention and by secondary memory, can be significantly reduced by consuming a low glycaemic index (GI) wholegrain breakfast, such as porridge, muesli or bran-enriched cereal, versus a high GI breakfast, such as white toast.

Other foods that have been shown to boost concentration include:

* Blueberries
* Water
* Dark chocolate
* Salmon
* Green tea
* Beets
* Bananas
* Spinach
* Eggs

Eat a Snack at 2pm

Eric Braverman (a New York physician and author of *The Edge Effect*) says that 2pm is when levels of serotonin (the brain chemical that helps regulate mood) can take a nosedive and that having a snack – ideally containing mood-boosting nutritional powerhouses like B vitamins (B6, B12 and folic acid) and complex carbs (whole grains) – will be most beneficial.

Focus With a Power Hour

When you are tired or stressed, or just finding it really hard to concentrate for long periods of time, try setting a specific amount of time (for example, one hour) that you can call your 'power hour'. Seeing an end in sight to your tasks, etc., can be very helpful for creating focus and creates a 'fake excitement' related for the task. Sometimes you have to play these tricks on your brain when you know what is good for it!

Personal Goals

Concentration is greatly aided by a clear direction. Knowing your goals every single day will dramatically support this. A useful model I often use with clients and myself is the GROW model.

This is a very useful model for setting direction and having a clear process for thinking about how you could achieve it. I try to self-coach every morning and focus on one or two main goals I have for that day. The key is to not overload yourself and to be realistic about your main goals. For example, I might use this in the following way:

Goal – I want to finish Chapter 9 of my book today.

Reality – I've already researched this area really well, so it's just a case of ordering the information and then personalising it.

Options – I could: a) chunk the day into three-hour slots using the first three hours for drafting, the second three hours for sense checking and the third three hours for a final draft, or b) just write freehand and see if this flows better, or c) divide the whole chapter into 10 logical sections and spend 45 minutes power writing each one!

Will – Knowing myself, I would probably work better with Option C, as the 'pressurised excitement' seems to work well for my style, so I will start with that. I'll give myself 30 minutes to familiarise myself with the research and divide it up then 45 minutes per section. Voila!

Another top tip is to state your *actions* and not just your *goals*. Goals can seem overwhelming, but actions feel easier to achieve. Stating your intended actions will therefore help with concentrating on the task of meeting your goals. For example, 'finish project' is a goal, but 'write first draft by today' and 'organise meeting to discuss content with Paul by Tuesday' are actions.

Staying Mindful

When you realise you are daydreaming, bring your attention back to the present moment. The more you do this, the easier it will become and the less your mind should wander. Eventually, you may find your mind is going through this process automatically, and without it having to consciously re-direct itself.

If you find you tend to drift off in meetings or lectures, try asking yourself questions as you're listening. For example:

- What is the topic about?
- What message is the speaker trying to convey?
- What are the main issues being discussed?

These types of questions will allow you to focus your attention on the conversation and away from any distractions.

Concentrating for long periods of time can be challenging, particularly for those with dyslexia. However, you have to remember that most people, dyslexic or not, will not remember every detail of a meeting, presentation or conversation, so relax – you are not alone!

Instead, try focusing on two or three main points to get an understanding of the overall message. It is also important to be as prepared as you can before any meeting so that you have some established 'mental hooks' on which to attach new information. Something as simple as knowing the agenda or the simple facts for each discussion point can greatly increase concentration.

Reading – If you find that you often 'drift off' whilst reading and don't remember what you have read, try stopping after each paragraph. The pause does not have to be long; just stop and ask yourself, 'What was the main point in this section?' or 'What did I just read?'.

This will reinforce what you have just read, re-focus your mind and save you time in the long run.

Desk Meditation

Meditation increases the thickness and strength of the frontal cortex of the brain. As we age, the frontal cortex decreases in size. Studies show that those who meditate experience less of this decrease in the frontal cortex. This is particularly true for brain areas associated with attention, perception and sensory processing.

It has been shown that meditation also improves efficiency via improved sustained attention and impulse control (Kozasa, 2011).

Simple approaches can include desk meditation which you can do for 5-10 minutes and don't need a mat! Try closing your eyes, releasing all thoughts about work, and just focus on deep breathing for a few minutes. If you find your mind starts to wander, just gently bring it back to the present moment.

Forget Multitasking – It's Cognitively Impossible!

You may be finding it hard to concentrate because you are trying to deal with several things in one go (a common problem in the modern-day workplace). However, research has shown that when participants tried to multitask, they simply worked at half the capacity (with one side of their brain working on one task and the other side working with another). Error rates also increased by 50%, which is rather worrying! (Koechlin, 2009). It turns out we are not multitasking but simply 'context switching' which slows us down.

Instead, aim to complete one task at a time and opt for 'stacking' similar tasks – e.g. focus on just email or phone calls at one time, so that you don't have to use too much brain power on switching between different activities.

De-Clutter

Researchers at the Princeton University Neuroscience Institute published the results of a study they conducted in *The Journal of Neuroscience* (January 2013) that unequivocally showed that:

> *'Multiple stimuli present in the visual field at the same time compete for neural representation by mutually suppressing their evoked activity throughout visual cortex, providing a neural correlate for the limited processing capacity of the visual system.'*

Or in other words, you can't focus when your environment is cluttered. Clutter means you get distracted, have reduced attention and leaves you unable to process information. Start by clearing your desk or by working in a clear, separate office when trying to complete complex tasks.

Chewing for Concentration

Researchers have found that chewing gum significantly increases concentration. In a controlled study, two groups were asked to listen to a 30-minute recording that included a sequence of numbers. One chewed gum and one did not chew gum during the recording. They found that the gum chewers had higher accuracy rates, maintained focus for longer and faster reaction times than the non-chewers. It is thought that the gum increases oxygen flow and can keep people more alert (*British Journal of Psychology*, 2013). The same seems to also apply for mints. This must be the easiest concentration strategy ever.

Concentration Reflector

Let's take a moment to consider the following strategy chart. Pick the top three strategies that would work for you. Remember to think about what you start doing today.

Habit/Technique	What Do I Need to Do or Try to Get Started?
Noise-cancelling Headphones	Cut out background noise with noise-cancelling headphones or your favourite music.
Desk Positioning	Reduce 360 noise by changing desk positions.
Alternate Physical Positions	Get up and move around frequently or stretch at your desk.
Work From Home	Try working from home one day a week or when working on complex, detailed work.
Manage Distractions From Others	Use standard sentences, set times or a traffic light system to decrease distractions and kindly let others know you are busy.
Technological Distractions	Turn off all pings, reminders and alerts to aid concentration on complex work.
Transposing Numbers	Get out your tracing paper to avoid errors!
Manage Your Energy Not Your Time	Consider your circadian rhythm and work out the best time of day for specific activities. Always complete routine tasks in your lowest energy times.
Cognitive Enhancers	Take regular breaks, holidays and exercise to improve concentration and productivity

Eating for Concentration	Ensure you have breakfast and then a snack at 2pm. Try including some of the concentration foods into your diet.
Create Excitement	Use power hours to trick your mind into a false sense of excitement and focus.
Stay Mindful	Practice bringing your awareness back to the room or subject with set questions and conscious thought.
Desk Meditation	Try desk meditation by closing your eyes and deep-breathing for five minutes.
Multitasking	Close down all of your multiple applications and focus on one task at a time.
Declutter	Clear your desk, create a clutter-free environment or move to a different space to free your mind of all visual stimuli.
Chew for Concentration	Increase oxygen to the brain by chewing gum before complex work.

Chapter 8

Procrastination and Prioritisation

'I'm not a procrastinator, I just enjoy stress-induced panic.'

– Anonymous

From my work with thousands of clients, I have my own personal theory that procrastination is just one of three things: being tired, being bored, or being overwhelmed. The great thing about this theory is that it has allowed my clients to be able to pinpoint the key issue and come up with an appropriate and effective strategy, instead of just saying they are procrastinators. It enables them to say, 'I procrastinate, because…'

In this chapter, we will cover these three areas and explore the following strategies for addressing them:

Overwhelmed Procrastination

- Visual Mapping
- Perfect Week Planning
- Managing Emails Effectively
- Prioritising – Eisenhower Box

- Stop Waiting for the Stars to Align
- Procrastination Busting Language

Tired Procrastination

- Working to Your Own Circadian Rhythms.
- Cognitive Enhancers
- Slow Releasing Energy Food
- Adjusting Bed and Wake Times

Bored Procrastination

- Reward – Washing Machine Time
- Verbal Commitments
- Changing Your Environment
- Hanging out With Inspiring People
- Procrastinating on Purpose

Overwhelmed Procrastination

Visual Mapping

Dyslexic individuals often have very good perceptual abilities and are very creative. Therefore, you might find it easier to remember things visually when organising activities. For example, to prevent over-whelmed procrastination, it is useful to employ colour to separate the tasks – for example, red for urgent tasks, amber for important tasks and green for non-urgent tasks.

Mind-mapping software (such as MindJet or MindMeister) can be a helpful tool for organising activities and planning projects. Mind-mapping software is a comprehensive tool that simplifies brainstorming, note taking and planning, and that visually reduces the complexity of tasks and projects. Text, notes, images and hyperlinks can be easily created, managed and added to the mind map, which allows the user to gain a holistic view of their work. This makes it easier to prioritise and order the objectives and tasks.

Perfect Week Planning

A good strategy for structuring workload is to break down the working week so that you have a clear record of what needs to be completed that week and by when it needs to be completed, so that you can plan your days accordingly.

One way to do this is to allocate 20 minutes at the beginning of each Monday morning. Take that time to list all of the things that need to be done that week, and then place them in order of importance with the expected time you will need to complete them. You can then create a 'perfect week schedule', which has all of the activities clearly organised.

Once the perfect week plan has been created, it is helpful to allocate an additional 10 minutes at the end of each day to review:

- The days' work – i.e., what you completed that day
- Outstanding work that you have accomplished
- Amendments to the timeline or importance of each task
- Any issues that might need to be discussed with a supervisor
- New or unexpected tasks

Manager Input – some people find it beneficial to schedule a meeting with their manager at the beginning and end of the week. This allows both people to discuss the work that has been completed during the week, the work that is going to be completed and any potential issues that need to be addressed. This form of open communication promotes support and healthy working relationships as well as work clarity.

Managing Emails Effectively

For most people, email takes up an enormous amount of their daily time and can be the thing that causes them to feel the most overwhelmed. Sometimes it doesn't matter how much you plan, emails will keep diverting attention away from whatever you're doing. A great strategy is to turn off the function that automatically sends alerts when you get a new email and schedule a set time once or twice a day to read and answer your emails. This will help clear up space for other tasks and enable you to give your full attention to the task at hand.

People with dyslexia may need to be more conscious of email distraction if they are prone to becoming disorganised or overwhelmed with a lot of information. A large inbox will also require heavy processing skills and working memory resources, so it is important to find effective strategies for staying in control of and processing incoming emails.

Another way of dealing with email overload is to assign emails from particular people or companies into specific folders such as *Client* or *Level of Importance*. This will help prioritise which emails need to be attended to immediately, which can wait and which can be disregarded. The emails can then be read in groups, making them more manageable to process.

A simple solution that I use is the Three Ds model:

- **D**o it – reply immediately if that can be done
- **D**elegate it – organise it into a folder to do later (see below)

- **D**elete it – delete it out of your inbox and free up your mental capacity

In addition to specific folders that you might already have, such as company, client, or departmental folders, I always have three separate folders:

- **Archive** – for everything I want to get out of my inbox but don't want to delete altogether

- **Reading** – for all of those non-urgent, FYIs and information that might be useful to read at a later date (which isn't urgent)

- **Follow-Up** – for emails/contacts that I may want to follow up at a later date, but have been dealt with at present and don't need to be in my inbox

Scannable Inboxes

An inbox should contain no more than 20 to 30 emails, because it should only include items that are awaiting a reply or action. 20 to 30 is a good number, because the content is quickly 'scannable'. This stops incessant and repeated reading of the same emails.

Breathe!

'Email apnea' is a new term to describe how people will often hold their breath whilst reading emails (probably due to feeling under pressure). Try and be aware of this and ensure that you are feeding your brain plenty of oxygen. This will ensure that you have the cognitive resources available to you to complete the task as efficiently and as quickly as you can.

Prioritisation – The Eisenhower Box

A timeless model for prioritisation is the Eisenhower Box of urgent vs important. Map all of your tasks to understand which need to be completed straight away and which can be scheduled for later or deleted entirely.

The Eisenhower Box

	Urgent	Not Urgent
Important	**Do** *Do it now.*	**Decide** *Schedule a time to do it.*
Not Important	**Delegate** *Who can do it for you?*	**Delete** *Eliminate it.*

Stop Waiting for the Stars to Align

My brother and I will often joke about how he likes the 'stars to be aligned' before he can start a new get-fit regime and I always tell him the same thing – the stars will never align. There is no such thing as the perfect day for action. You will not suddenly wake up and know how to 'adult'. Big things get achieved through small, consistent efforts. Start today, no matter how small. Grab a coffee and put together a plan, map out some ideas and spend ten minutes today thinking about your plan of attack on something. The small win will inspire more action.

Procrastination Busting Language – No More Weasel Words!

Watch out for language that allows you to avoid dealing with things such as:

- I can't
- I would, but
- I'll *try* to do it
- Maybe
- Potentially
- Possibly
- Maybe

We have a great phrase for these in psychology – weasel words. They are words that allow you to wriggle and hide without committing to anything! *Star Wars* hero Yoda famously said, 'Do or do not, there is no try!'

Change your language, change your mindset. Try using these words instead:

- I can
- I will
- I am able to
- I am free
- I have time
- I can achieve this by
- I am going to

Not only will you feel a sudden sense of empowerment, but you are more likely to achieve your goals, as the language normally precedes a more tangible plan.

Also, be aware of your 'catastrophising' language:

- This is going to be terrible
- I'll get this wrong
- Everyone will laugh
- I'll just die if I get this wrong!

In the great words of the 19th century poet and philosopher Ralph Waldo Emerson:

> 'Watch your thoughts, for they become words. Choose your words, for they become actions. Understand your actions, for they become habits. Study your habits, for they will become your character. Develop your character, for it becomes your destiny.'

Tired Procrastination

Circadian Rhythms

Obviously, if you are tired, you may be more prone to procrastinate, so consider your circadian rhythm (discussed in the previous chapter) to ensure that you are working to your own natural energy levels throughout the day.

Breaks

If you are finding that you cannot complete a task and are wasting a lot of time, then don't fight it. Go for a break or at least start another task and come back to the difficult one later. Sometimes our brains just need to stop analysing the problem and they will become more responsive and better able to handle the problem after we have stopped trying and have devoted our attention to something else for a short time.

Consider Your Food Options

Try eating slow energy releasing foods for breakfast, such as porridge, which will give you a more consistent level of glucose throughout the day. Avoid heavy sandwiches, cakes, or other carbohydrate-heavy foods at lunchtime. These foods might release a sugar 'hit' but they will send your energy and mental stamina crashing later in the afternoon.

Sleep and Wake Times

Keeping regular sleep and wake times is easier said than done with our 24-hour lives, but make a conscious effort to have set times when you go to sleep and wake up in the morning. This will make it easier for you to work out your natural energy levels throughout the day and therefore plan your tasks accordingly.

Removing electronic equipment from your bedroom is hugely helpful. If you find this too difficult, then try at least to have your phone on the other side of the room and commit to a 'cut-off time' for using it.

Bored Procrastination

Reward – Washing Machine Time

One of the main ways you can trick your mind into enjoying a task is to set yourself a challenge, and then reward yourself at its end. I previously mentioned creating fake excitement through a 'Power Hour'. In addition to this, I personally have an idea called 'Washing

Machine Time' that I will often employ personally. I will set myself the challenge of completing a boring task in the time that the washing machine takes to complete a cycle. You'll be amazed at just how effective this actually is (silly, but effective!). I then give myself a reward (normally food-based) to create a new, neural pathway in my brain that tricks my brain into thinking the task is more exciting than it actually is.

Verbal Commitments

The simple act of sharing your goals for the next hour, afternoon, etc. with someone else makes you commit to that task with a whole new level of enthusiasm. Not only is talking your ideas through with someone else helpful for planning and time management purposes, there is a great motivational benefit to bringing someone else in on your plan, because you will have an outside incentive to complete it. That incentive might be the reinforcement of approval, or just that you don't want someone else to think that you failed, but either way, it works.

Change Your Environment

As the old adage goes, 'A change is as good as a rest.' If your working environment does not inspire you, then move. How we feel about our surroundings makes a huge difference to our boredom levels. Personally, I rather enjoy working at coffee shops where the table is clear of anything that could distract me in the office, but I still have access to stimulation.

Hang Out With Inspiring People

I once read that you're the average of the five people you hang out with most, which always mildly amused me. I do think this is true, however.

Find people who inspire you to action, whether this is colleagues, friends or inspiring bloggers.

Procrastinate on Purpose

The idea of procrastinating on purpose means not completing a specific task right away but thinking about it in some conscious way over time. There has been a suggestion that this can lead to more creativity, but the jury is still out on this one! The idea being, though, that sometimes we are so overwhelmed, tired or bored that starting the task is just too much but if we put it off in a conscious way, we might be able to access different ideas from those if we just completed it quickly.

Try this by loosely planning ideas or providing a structure to the task on a small scale (perhaps as bullet points or a visual diagram). Frequently revisit the notes and see if your ideas for the task start improving with time.

Procrastination Reflector

Let's take a moment to reflect on the techniques listed in this chapter. Pick the top three strategies that would work for you. Remember to think about what you start doing today.

Habit/Technique	What Do I Need to Do or Try to Get Started?
Overwhelmed Procrastination	
Visual Mapping	Use mind-mapping to prevent overwhelmed procrastination and allow for everything to be clearly seen.

Perfect Week Planning	Consider what a perfect schedule would look like at the beginning of each week and plan each accordingly with the regular manager check-ins.
Manage Emails Effectively	Spend time creating simple email habits such as checking at set times and organising work into specific files such as Archive, Reading & Follow-Up.
Scannable Inboxes	Ensure that you have no more than 20-30 emails in your inbox at any one time so that it is 'scannable'. This will take an initial organising stage but will ensure that only 'current/unanswered' emails are waiting in your inbox.
Prioritisation	Use the Eisenhower Box to understand the urgency/importance of all of your tasks to encourage prioritisation and avoid feeling overwhelmed with knowing where to start.
Stop Waiting for the Stars to Align	Take action today with small conscious efforts instead of waiting for the perfect day for organising.
Procrastination-Busting Language	Avoid using weasel words like 'try', 'maybe' and 'can't' and replace them with phrases such as 'I will,' and 'I can achieve this by'. Watch out for the 'catastrophising' language..

Tired Procrastination

Working to Your Own Circadian Rhythm	Adapt your day to own natural energy levels. Routine tasks should be carried out in your lowest energy times, leaving your highest energy times for the more cerebral tasks!

Breaks	Don't forget to rename breaks 'cognitive enhancers' to remind you how their powerful effects and then schedule them regularly. Create that habit every day.
Slow Energy Foods	Avoid heavy sandwiches, cakes and carbs at lunchtime to maximise your energy in the afternoon.
Bed and Wake Times	Create a habit of having the same bedtime. Set an alarm on your phone for bedtime and rise times. It's amazing how that little nudge can help encourage the habit.

Bored Procrastination

Reward – Washing Machine Time	Using an external device to create 'fake excitement' and force you into completing a task in a specific timeframe.
Verbal Commitments	Share your goal with someone else to ensure you have committed to the cause. Make sure they check up on you!
Change Your Environment	Experiment with different workplaces – e.g. coffee shops, a library or at home, to discover where you get the biggest 'buzz'.
Hang Out With Inspiring People	Make sure you get a regular dose of optimistic, inspiring people that will encourage you to push yourself further. Dump the doom-goblins!
Procrastinate on Purpose	For complex or large tasks, draft some notes or a mind-map then put it somewhere you can see over the coming days or weeks to ensure that you are procrastinating with a purpose!

My Dyslexia – Real Life Case Study D

Name: Peter B
Profession: CEO
Years in Role: 8

When did you realise you thought differently?
I found out I was dyslexic when I was about seven years old. My brother, who is four years older than me, is dyslexic, so they tested me just in case.

I am not sure I realised I thought differently until quite recently. I have always struggled with spelling, and reading used to be a problem, but now I am much better. I only realised I thought differently after I got married about five years ago. My wife just sits with her mouth open when I explain how I made a decision. She thinks I should have taken another 30 steps before reaching the conclusion I made.

What are your strengths?
Enterprise, hard work, energy, enthusiasm, determination and table tennis.

What are your weaknesses?
Quick thinking. I am always saying to myself, 'I wish I had said that' after an event.

I am also not good at spelling or thinking laterally. If you put me under time pressure, I am shocking.

I remember a director of a famous firm of occupational psychologists did not offer me a job because, in his words: 'You being dyslexic is difficult. We really liked you, but we just do not have the time to be re-doing your work all the time.' I know now that what he said was illegal, but to be honest, I had heard similar things all through my life. It didn't really cross my mind until just recently what a terrible thing that was to say to someone with a disability.

What are the best things about being dyslexic/neuro-diverse?
I guess the enterprise bit. I also don't worry about making mistakes because I made so many as a kid, it just became second nature.

What are your top strategies that help you work better?
WORK HARDER. Check, re-check and then re-check again any work that goes to a client. I know it will not be right first time, so there is no point in sending it straight away. You have to realise that your education is to prepare you for life. It should not negatively affect you for the rest of your life. If you didn't do well at school, so what? That should not define you for the rest of your life.

At age 16, I got three GCSEs. I had to re-sit, and then only got one more. My confidence was shot. It was not until I moved school (for the second time) that a teacher said to me and my dad, 'Do you realise Peter is very clever? He is one of the brightest children I have had in years. His dyslexia has caused him to lose his confidence. He needs to work harder and stop worrying about making mistakes.'

Within six weeks, I completed a GCSE in Maths and got 95% – a B grade on the intermediary level exam. I then got A, B and C at A-Level, a 2:1 in Psychology from Surrey and a merit in my MSc in Occupational Psychology from Birkbeck. I am now a chartered occupational psychologist (a doctorate-level qualification) and am an Associate Fellow of the British Psychological Society.

I started my own company, and within five years, we had turned over £4m. I now employ 12 people. It will probably all go to shit sometime soon, but hey, that just means you have to pick yourself back up and go again!

Anything else you would like to say about it?
I think it has actually been a gift to me: a thorn in my side that has driven me to do well.

Chapter 9

Written Communication

'If you want to be a writer, you must do two things above all others: read a lot and write a lot.'

– Stephen King

In this chapter we will cover tips for:

* Spelling
* Structuring Information
* Proof-reading
* Meeting Notes

Spelling

Auditory (Sound) Spellcheckers – Auditory spellcheckers allow the user to phonetically (spelling them as they sound) spell words, which makes finding the word in the first place much easier. It also enables the user to hear the words they are trying to spell, ensuring they are using the word they intended and reducing the risk of confusion between words that visually look similar.

Software – Text Help software has a homophone spellcheck ('homo' = 'same', 'phone' = 'sound', so words that sound the same but look different) which is more advanced than the generic spell check on Word and can help pick out typical phonetic errors within a document.

Tools for Handwritten Work – There are many forms of spell checkers, both for phones and computers. However, this does not help when having to hand-write documents. The Quicktionary Super Pen Professional scans writing, spellchecks it, then reads the words out loud and provides a definition. This allows the user to check that they are using the right word and that it is spelt correctly.

Job-Specific Word Lists – For a more cost-effective strategy, some may find it beneficial to keep a notebook with common job-specific spellings and phrases. This makes it quick and easy to refer to when writing documents and emails.

Games – Spelling often improves with practice. Therefore, it can help to use games available online to reinforce spelling skills and learn how to spell particular words. For example, a good option is Starspell, where every word is spoken and many have pictures. It is also possible with Starspell to create personal word lists and subject-specific vocabularies.

Structuring Information and Planning Written Work

Templates – If you feel that you struggle with report writing or writing to clients, it is a good idea to raise that issue with your manager. You might consider asking your manager to provide you with a template for commonly produced written work, and with a list of key terms, phrases, or points that need to be included in a particular document.

Bullet points – A helpful strategy is to write bullet points detailing what it is you want to convey in whatever you are writing. This will provide you with a structure for your document and a point of reference to ensure you have included everything you aimed to cover. When possible, use bullet points to convey your message, such as when you are sending an email to a client. Bullet points allow you to make your point clear. For example, you could open your letter with bullets before attending to complex, detailed information as follows:

Dear Ray,
I am writing to give you an update on the following:

- *The 2022 Project*
- *Who will be involved*
- *Dates and timings of key meetings*
- *Training venues*
- *Your research*

I wanted to let you know where we are so far with the new project. We are calling this the 2022 Project as it is following our 2022 strategic plan.
At present, we have Clare, Leah, Jonathan, Emma and David involved and we will probably also include Tina and Martin.
We have already considered dates and timings which are April 22, May 26th, June 25th, July 27th and August 30th. Please let me know you are in agreement with these as we will need to book venues and arrange

the necessary refreshments etc.

We also need to discuss how we will use your research as I think there is a direct link with the work we have been doing in the past year. We might want to give this some careful consideration as I think it would be a useful addition to the project report.

PROVE Model – The PROVE model is a very effective way to structure a document and can give a useful framework for most documents.

- Position – start with your position/main point

- Reason – outline one to three of your most compelling reasons

- Other View – outline how you have considered the reader's point of view

- Verify – consider what evidence you have for your viewpoint

- End – summarise the key points and next steps

Know, Feel, Do – It's also useful to consider what you want the reader to Know, Feel, Do following reading your document. Most people focus on one or two of these areas and not all three. Consideration of these can dramatically change the reader experience.

Mind-mapping Software – An excellent tool for structuring documents. It allows the user to create documents in a more visual and creative way, and then later to turn them into linear documents appropriate for the workplace.

Transcribing Software – Speech recognition software such as Dragon Naturally Speaking transcribes audio information and allows the user to dictate anything he or she wants to write, such as reports, emails and notes. This software comes with a spell checker. It has advanced technology that picks up job-specific terms and predicts their use, which helps the user write appropriately in different professional contexts.

Proof-reading

Here are my top tips for proof-reading:

- Only proof-read when rested and always wait for a day or two after completing large documents to revisit them.

- Read it out loud *and* also silently.

- Check for homonyms which are words that sound the same but are spelt very differently like 'there' and 'their' or 'weather' and 'whether'.

- Read it backwards to focus on the spelling of words.

- Check numbers – e.g. £20,000 and £200,000.

- Read it slowly for accuracy and quickly for tone.

- Point with your finger to read one word at a time.

- Do one proof for spelling, another for missing/additional spaces, consistency of word usage, font sizes, etc.

- Keep a list of your most common spelling/punctuation or grammatical errors.

- Use the 'Track Changes' function in Word to make your comments apparent to other reviewers.

- Proof-read from a hard copy as well as the screen.

- Give a copy of the document to another person and take turns in reading different sections.

- Proof-read several times, preferably on different days.

- Closely review page numbers and other footer/header material for accuracy and correct order.

Text-to-Speech Software – As previously mentioned, this allows you to hear your work read back to you, which is excellent for proof-reading and checking sentence structure and overall layout.

Writing Meeting Notes

Handwriting Translation Pen – Using a handwriting translation pen, such as the Livescribe 3 Smart Pen, can be useful, as it automatically converts handwritten notes into text on your computer. This ensures that all of your information gets stored on one device. It saves you from having to look through old notebooks and scraps of paper for conventionally written notes, by putting those notes directly into computer texts when they are first written. The pen also has an audio record function, which allows you to record any key information you would like to remember, or that you may have forgotten to write down.

Written Communication Reflector

Let's take a moment to reflect on the techniques listed in this chapter. Pick the top three strategies that would work for you. Remember to think about what you start doing today.

Habit/Technique	What Do I Need to Do or Try to Get Started?
Spelling	
Auditory Spell-checkers	Spellcheckers that allow you to phonetically check your spelling.
Text Help	Text-to-speech software which allows you to 'hear' what's on the screen. Great for proofreading your own work and comprehension.
Quicktionary Pen	A device which scans writing, spellchecks it, then reads the words out loud and provides a definition.
Word Lists	Keep a list of job-specific words or phrases that you commonly use to reduce errors and to improve your memory of them.
Games	Starspell offers a more fun way to improve spelling ability.

Structuring

Bullet or Numbered Points	Bullet points are a great way of providing clarity and an easy way to signpost what you are about to discuss next in a document.
PROVE Model	Position, Reason, Other View, Verify and End. Use this simple method to structure all proposals and arguments.
Know, Feel, Do	Remember what you want your target audience/reader to know, feel and do following your idea/proposal.
Mind-mapping Software	The software is an excellent way of emptying all of your thoughts in a creative and user-friendly way before you decide on the structure, which can also be done visually.
Transcribing Software	If you find it easier to talk than type, try using voice-to-text that will allow you to transcribe all of your ideas without typing a word!
Proof-reading Tips	Write one tip below that you will start using from today.
Meeting Notes – Handwriting Translation Pen	A wonderful invention allowing your hand-written notes to be cleverly converted into text on your computer.

Chapter 10

Reading Comprehension

'*To read without reflecting, is like eating without digesting.*'
— *Edmund Burke*

In this chapter we will cover tips for:

- Text-to-speech for Comprehension
- SQ3R Technique
- Skimming
- Scanning

Text-to-speech Software

Text-to-speech software (as previously mentioned) is a great tool for helping you *understand* what you are reading. It works by reading selected written text aloud. This can increase comprehension a great deal by allowing the user to focus on the material, rather than on the act of reading.

Smartphones have a great feature which works just like the text-to-speech software. For iPhone users: Turn on 'Speak' mode, highlight the subject text on your phone (i.e. a document or email) and the function will read the text out loud.

SQ3R Technique

If you often get lost when reading large documents or articles, a good strategy is to make a list of the key points or ideas for which you are looking. This should minimise the chances of getting confused or having to re-read the document several times. Additionally, it may help you to stop at the end of each chapter or section and write down the key points (either as bullet points or as a small summary). This will make it more difficult to forget what you have just read.

In the 1940s Francis Robinson developed a method known as the SQ3R. This method was designed to help individuals: (1) think about what information they want to get from a document, (2) decide on the appropriate level of attention needed and (3) remember what they have read. This method was originally developed as an effective study technique. It has since been more widely applied to almost every learning situation, including the workplace.

SQ3R stands for Scan, Question and the Three Rs – Read, Remember, Review:

1. **Scan** – Skim the text quickly for key words, do not ignore any illustrations, diagrams or graphs. Remember that important information is often highlighted in a text box or in bold or italics. Does this text give you the information you are looking for or do you need to look for a different source?

2. **Question** – Ask yourself what information you hope to get from your reading and how this information will help you. By questioning the material, you are more likely to engage with it and therefore more likely to retain the information.

3. **Read** – Read the text one section at a time. Here, it is important to

make notes or highlight key information and anything you don't understand and that you may need to clarify.

4. **Remember** – Run through the section you have read, focusing on key and relevant information, and try to summarise and articulate your understanding. Use this time to work out how other information you have read fits around it.

5. **Review** – Read the document or your notes again to check if you have remembered information correctly. When possible, discuss the information you have learnt with someone else. This is a great way to show that you understand what you have read.

Tip: Use mind-maps to record important information. You can then add to this with information from other documents. This will make it easier to build a full, visual picture of whatever you are researching.

Skimming

Skimming is an excellent technique to help you get an overview of the main focus of the argument before you focus on the detail. There are two popular techniques:

1. **Start-finish**: This method is based on the idea that most texts will have an introduction, body and conclusion. Based on this structure, the key information should be presented three times:

- A brief overview in the introduction
- A detailed description and evaluation in the main body
- A review/summary in the conclusion

The idea behind this method, therefore, is to read the first and last (concluding) paragraph of each chapter or section of the document to get an idea of what the author is going to cover, and to determine whether the information is of interest to you.

2. **First sentences**: This method is based on the assumption that the main points of each paragraph will be introduced in the opening sentence. To gain an understanding of the main arguments and structure of the text, try reading only the first sentence of each paragraph. Once you have determined whether the paragraph is relevant, then you can either read the full text or disregard it and move on to the next.

Both of these methods are designed to help you get a broad overview of the material and save you from wasting time reading irrelevant text or documents. Moreover, using these skimming techniques will give you a basic understanding of the text and its underlying message when you come to read the full text.

Scanning

Scanning, on the other hand, is useful in helping you identify or locate in a large or complicated text specific information such as a name, date, statistic, or important fact. Scanning can save you time from having to read entire documents for one or two specific bits of information. This will also reduce the chances of you getting over-whelmed by irrelevant information and forgetting what it was you wanted to gain from the text. When scanning:

- **Be clear about what you are searching for**: Write your topics down so that you can refer to the list when scanning to avoid getting distracted by other less important information. Alternatively, try picturing the statistic, name, or fact in your mind to help you focus your attention when searching.

- **Anticipate what form the information is likely to be in**: If it is a statistic, will it be represented in a table or graph? If it is a name, is it more likely to be in the text or in the footnotes?

- **Identify what kind of text it is**: If it is a fairly short or easy-to-read document, you can consider scanning the entire document. If it is a lengthy or complex work such as a book or a scientific journal, consider skimming first to identify which parts of the text you will scan.

- **Make it easy on yourself**: When reading large documents for the first time, it can help to use the Ctrl+F function on your computer. This allows the reader to search for key information in the document. In doing this, you can find terms quickly and determine the relevance of the document efficiently. You can also access the relevant information without getting lost in the detail. This will also allow you to disregard the document if it is irrelevant or not useful, without wasting hours actually reading through it.

Reading Comprehension Reflector

Let's take a moment to reflect on the techniques listed in this chapter. Pick the top three strategies that would work for you. Remember to think about what you start doing today.

Habit/Technique	What Do I Need to Do or Try to Get Started?
Text-to-speech Software	This software allows you to have the text read to you, thereby allowing you to focus more on the content and meaning than the physical act of reading.
SQ3R	Scan, Question, Read, Remember, Review is a simple approach that gives you a clear method for reading any document.
Skimming	Use the 'start-finish' or 'first-sentence' approach to skim for key information at specific points in the document. This can really help pinpoint where you are likely to find your key information.
Scanning	Scanning is an effective way to reduce the reading time involved in large documents. Just be sure to write down what exactly you are looking for, where you might find it and use Ctrl+F to scan for specific information or trigger words that may be useful.

My Dyslexia – Real Life Case Study E

Name: Brendan N
Profession: Research Officer
Years in Role: 3

When did you realise you thought differently?
At college. I always thought I was stupid. My father and two brothers had experienced the same thing. Our school had treated us all as if we were stupid, and we accepted that. Despite this, we enjoyed talking about intellectual subjects. My dad would talk about ideas I had been learning in college despite his having dropped out of school. During one such discussion in a pub, it occurred to me that we weren't born stupid. We were born with a different way of thinking. We thought creatively; we learned through discussion and not by writing or reading.

What are your strengths?
I think my greatest strength is being open-minded. I try to think around problems, looking at them from lots of angles. This means I often come up with unusual solutions. My day-to-day work demands creativity and being open-minded gives me an ability to do this in spades. I have an interest in people, and I like to listen rather than talk. I am a quiet person. My dyslexia discourages me to speak, but there is much to be said about having an ability to listen and consider the thoughts of others.

What are your weaknesses?
I suffer in terms of speed, as things take me longer. For me, tasks need

to be well planned, checked and double-checked. My work quality can drop when I am forced to rush, and my dyslexic tendencies like to surface when the stress builds. I also find my concentration can be problematic. There is also the spelling and slow processing speed. This is not a problem as I find it helps me understand things better, but it means I work that bit slower. I also find that when I am interrupted completing a task, it can take me some time to refocus.

What are the best things about being dyslexic/neuro-diverse?

I have never been asked what's good about being dyslexic. There are good things about it. It encourages you to be aware about yourself – see your strengths and weakness. My strengths come from being dyslexic. It shapes the way I think and so my ability to be open-minded and creative. I have become self-reflective and always look for ways to learn.

Strangely, I am a better reader because I am dyslexic. I was forced to learn the rules of English, my common mistakes and better ways to check over my work. I guess the best thing about being dyslexic is the satisfaction of overcoming the issues and seeing the results.

What are your top strategies that help you work better?

Planning: I find that being organised helps. Lists, diaries and notes keep me from forgetting things. The Outlook calendar has been a wonder, as it can keep track of people's names, numbers, email, events, deadlines and other things I tend to forget.

It also helps to leave time to practice and prepare for something, particularly when it involves reading, writing and speaking. I couldn't do a thing without planning and preparation.

Support: Lucky for me, I have three dyslexic family members, all of whom have been in the same situation as me. We help one another, and when the frustrations of dyslexia hit, there is a good place to vent. It also helps to have good people around when things get tough. I now have a dyslexic friend at work, and we chat about our various strategies. I have picked up some new ones to try out.

Mind Set: I try to not get worried about my problems and focus on my achievements. Learning that I wasn't stupid made a huge difference. I take pride in what I do, even if it's just writing a paragraph. I spend a moment to think 'I did well there'.

Anything else you would like to say about it?

When I was young, picking up a book was incredibly scary, and the thought of writing made me shiver. Having found coping strategies, I now find reading and writing incredibly satisfying. I started writing creatively and I intend to publish my own book or novel. The ideas buzz around my head and I want to express them.

The best thing is realising you're not worse than other people; you just think differently.

Chapter 11

Impact and Verbal Communication

'The only limit to your impact is your imagination and commitment.'
– Tony Robbins

According to the National Institute of Mental Health, UK '74 percent of us dread public speaking'. Although many dyslexic individuals will have high verbal communication skills, giving presentations involves a degree of organisation and structure with which many dyslexics struggle. The tips in this section might aid your presentation skills and improve your verbal communication.

In this chapter we will cover:

- Signposting/Banks of Standard Sentences
- Prompt Cards
- Storytelling
- Dictaphone
- Structuring Your Thoughts
- Focusing on Your Audience
- Practising Assertiveness not Aggression

Signposting With Banks of Standard Sentences

Signposting is a great strategy to use when giving a presentation. Having a bank of phrases such as 'Now I am going to explain/talk about ...' or 'So far, we have covered ... and I would like to move onto ...' can help structure the presentation. They will also give you time to compose yourself and think of what you want to say next.

Prompt Cards

Prompt cards are a great way to jog your memory during a presentation. It is best to keep your note cards simple and have short phrases and single words as reminders of what you need to say without writing down the whole presentation.

Storytelling

If you find that you often get muddled up in what you are saying when giving a speech or an interview, you may benefit from using the 'storytelling strategy'. Think of your content as telling a story. You will need to ensure that what you are saying has a clear beginning, middle and end. For example, describe in a narrative fashion what the situation was, what you did or how you came up with a solution, and what the result was. Following this structure will help you give appropriate responses and ensure that the listener understands what you are trying to say.

Storytelling also increases cortisol (to make us pay attention), oxytocin (to create empathy) and dopamine (to give us a feeling of reward). No wonder it works so well!

Dictaphones

Use a dictaphone or phone to record yourself when practising for a presentation. Hearing your own words aloud will help you notice any potential areas of difficulty, such as pausing or gaps in the material. You can then perfect your presentation and do more recorded trial runs to help impress the information into your mind and hear what the recipients will hear.

Use an Effective Structure – PROVE

When presenting an idea, solution, or proposal, you can also use the PROVE model to give you an effective structure and ensure you raise all critical points logically.

- Position – start with your position or main point

- Reason – outline one to three of your most compelling reasons

- Other View – outline how you have considered the reader's point of view

- Verify – consider what evidence you have for your viewpoint

- End – summarise the key points and next steps

Focusing on Your Audience

Before a discussion, try to think of any hesitations your colleague or client might have and be sure to include something in your 'pitch' that will appease their apprehensions.

- After you have finished, leave time for the individual(s) to process what you have said.

- Ask them what they think, and show that you respect their view.

- Keep emotions neutral and do not get angry if they are not completely convinced. Instead, compromise or offer a solution.

- Stop talking and allow time for listening. Listen with an open mind. Acknowledge the content and, if appropriate, nod your head in agreement. This will encourage the person to keep talking, and it shows that you are interested. This motivates others to continue thinking of ideas, and it increases productivity as it shows that their efforts are valued.

- Empathise by trying to put yourself in the listener's position. Mimic their facial responses. If they are happy, smile with them. If they are giving you some feedback, soften your facial expression to show you care. This builds rapport and creates trust in you.

Practice Assertiveness not Aggression

Assertiveness is not about getting your own way or forcing your views on others – that is aggressive. This does not mean that you have to bend to the will of others, or follow what others say blindly. Being that passive generally will not get you anywhere. Assertiveness is about gaining support and building rapport. This is done by standing up for your ideas, beliefs and proposals but also by respecting the views and opinions of the people around you.

Impact and Verbal Communication Reflector

Let's take a moment to reflect on the techniques listed in this chapter. Pick the top three strategies that would work for you.

Remember to think about what you start doing today.

Habit/Technique	What Do I Need to Do or Try to Get Started?
Signposting	Signposting your audience with standard sentences that you have already in your mind 'bank' can be an excellent way of structuring your talk and reducing the cognitive load on your brain of trying to formulate new sentences!
Prompt Cards	Use small cards with a few words on each subject is a great mental trigger when under pressure and still looks very professional.
Storytelling	It is easy to remember a story with a start, middle and end that a list of information points. Practising the 'story' beforehand will also allow you to add mental visuals cues to help you remember when you go live.
Dictaphone	Record yourself when rehearsing your topic to allow you to hear what it sounds like in reality then refine and re-do.
PROVE Model	Use the Position, Reason, Other View, Verify and End model to ensure a powerful, structured presentation.
Focus on Your Audience	Think of the needs of your audience and after your discussion, think about the specific questions they may have, ask them to reflect and ensure you listen to them.
Practice Assertiveness not Aggression	Remember, true assertiveness is respecting the rights of your opinion and the other person's. Aggression is only respecting your own.

Interesting Neuroscience – Physiological Confidence

Did You Know?

Research from Harvard University (2012) demonstrated that it was possible to trick your brain into believing you are more confident. By creating specific 'power poses' such as spreading your arms and legs out wide for just two minutes at a time (don't try this on the London Underground), you can physiologically trick your brain into producing 25% more testosterone (fight mode – which is good for confidence) and 20% less cortisol (flight mode – which makes you want to run away), which makes you feel all round more confident. Yes, we think that's rather amazing too.

So, arms and legs wide, stretch out for a few minutes at the beginning of the day, or before that stressful meeting, and you can physiologically improve your confidence!

My Dyslexia – Real Life Case Study F

Name: Oonagh O
Profession: Curriculum Leader
Years in Role: 8

When did you realise you thought differently?
Very early on, I didn't like large social situations such as parties and school. I found it extremely stressful and wanted to just be with my mum. I don't know if it is related, but I also hid from getting my photo taken until I was about 12.

I quite often wanted to play on my own and make up stories. I loved running and drawing. I loved making up stories but knew my writing and spelling was different than everyone else's. As school went on, I found it extremely stressful, because anything that I had to do on rote, like times tables or vocabulary for languages, I just couldn't do. I knew I wasn't stupid, but I found some things very difficult and I seemed to worry more than anyone. As a child, I worried about everything and thought I would grow out of it.

What are your strengths?
I think I am good at reading people and noticing small things. I am good at having ideas and coming up with them really quickly. I can make people laugh.

What are your weaknesses?
Always presuming something is about me and about how I can't do things. I am very negative about myself.

What are the best things about being dyslexic/neuro-diverse?
I think I have been very confused about the conflict or apparent extreme differences in my character. I could do some things really well and felt very confident in them, and then other apparently easy things I couldn't do and I just thought I was useless. Now I think I understand that I actually have some strengths, and they didn't happen by luck or fluke (the success of my books). They are real and they aren't in any way 'diluted' just because I also do some things badly. Essentially, that it is possible to be really good at some things and really bad at other things. It doesn't make it 'not real' or mean that you are a fraud.

What are your top strategies that help you work better?
Mine is very practical. I now put everything in my calendar on my phone with alerts, and I keep a 'live' document of things to do on my phone notes. It takes away a lot of anxiety, and I can delete things out as I do them or print it in hard copy.

I also do this with an ideas page. I also have certain cues in my notes so I can remember things like names, etc. on my phone.

Anything else you would like to say about it?
This has really changed my life. I feel I have battled with terrible insecurities and anxiety and as a result depression, due to feeling as though I didn't really understand myself. The basic analogy I can give is like being a fantastic sprinter and everyone saying that you are lying because you can't run a marathon.

I think very early on I realised I was feeling and reacting to situations, and due to maybe being dismissed, not understanding it myself, or being ignored, it grew into huge self-doubt and negativity. The most intense thing about finding out I was dyslexic is that all my work has been rooted in this confusion. All my work is about people, desire (for example, looking at things you have dismissed and how we can make them desirable) and identities, including fake, counterfeit, or duplicate identities.

It has, as a result, been a very emotional experience, as I know there was some discussion about me potentially being dyslexic at age 10, but again it was dropped because I was doing well at school. I wonder what I would be like if I had been screened back then. This is not with regret, but I do wonder if I would have had less depression in my life, because I may have built strategies to deal with the initial thoughts that there was something wrong with me.

Chapter 12

Managing Others

Understanding Personality Effects on Your Performance

'Be grateful for the difficult people in your life, for they have shown you exactly who you don't want to be!'

– Anonymous

As previously mentioned in Chapter 5, we all have different personality types, and there will be a number of ways that your colleagues (because of their personality type – not just because they're trying to annoy you), will be stealing your time. Whilst it is very hard to get rid of these distractions altogether (and who would want to?), it is important to be clever about how you manage them.

Refer to Chapter 5 for a summary of the summary of the personality types. For example:

Highly conscientious people may take your time by constantly seeking clarification, perhaps from their need to get it right. Be clear at the outset about what you expect, by when, and when the check-in points will be, and they will be less likely to fear getting it wrong. Low conscientiousness people, on the other hand, may not give *enough* consideration to detail and process.

Highly agreeable people may overly worry and may need assurance. Give them regular positive feedback and ensure they understand how they are contributing to the overall success of the project and to the team. By contrast, low agreeableness people may be very happy to challenge you and to discuss the matter if they don't like something!

People high on the openness to experience scale – will take your time by constantly coming up with new ideas or changing an approach halfway through. Be clear early on about what you expect from them. Give them set deadlines, otherwise it won't get done. Channel their creativity by ensuring that they consider their new idea in terms of practicality. Give them set times for their ideas such as a weekly slot in a meeting and be firm that this is the time you will discuss new ideas. Low open to experience people, on the other hand, may not want to try a new way of doing things.

Managing Others Reflector

Consider who you have on your team and what effects their personality has on the way you work.

What do you need to do to minimise the distractions from them?

Neuroscience Research – How We React to Others

In the late 1990s, the scientist Rizzolatti accidentally discovered what were later termed 'mirror neurons'. Neurons are nerve cells, which can send messages from one part of the brain to another. Today we have dozens of ways to send messages (phone, email) and dozens of types of messages (Viber, WhatsApp). Neurons are similar in that there are different ways of transferring messages and different types of messages they transfer.

One type is mirror neurons. Mirror neurons cover large areas of the cerebral cortex, particularly the motor regions (which deal with our movement) (Dumas, 2010). They are extraordinary in that they fire (send messages) not only when an individual is performing an action, but also when an individual is watching someone else perform an action. This was a huge breakthrough in neuroscience because it showed that our brains have the ability to mirror the neural activation of an action just by watching it. Soon after, researchers also discovered that we are able to simulate other people's emotions and the intentions behind their actions. But what does this have to do with work environments?

Our brains' ability to mirror the neural activation of other peoples' actions and emotions extends to negative ones, such as fear, anxiety and stress. Researchers have found that just by looking at fearful faces, our brains stimulate the amygdala (which is the area that regulates emotion), activating the fear response. What's more is that this response was present even when individuals were not consciously aware that they had been shown a fearful face. **This demonstrates that we are largely affected by the people around us** (Ghadiri et al., 2012).

Although we may not be conscious that the fear response has been activated, our performance at work can be adversely affected:

1. **Fear or stress have a negative effect on the hormonal balance** between the body and the brain. Long-term fear or stress leads to burnout.

2. The amygdala is directly connected to the prefrontal cortex (PFC) where many of our executive functions lie (executive functions include our working memory, which we know can be weaker already, before we add stress!). An over-active amygdala can inhibit the PFC, thus **reducing our ability to think rationally and balance information.** Moreover, it inhibits the dorsolateral PFC, which is responsible for short-term memory storage (Petrides, 2010), therefore limiting our ability to deal with complexity and change.

3. The **amygdala also activates the fight-or-flight response and** leads to an increase in energy. This was once thought to be a desirable response and was often used as a method of motivating employees. Today, however, we know the following:

- Fear – can lead to aggressive, protective behaviour, which counteracts collaborative, team-working activities

- Flight – can result in individuals ignoring work or choosing not to deal with issues that require great effort

Therefore, fear reduces a person's productivity either through thoughtless actions or inactivity, both of which negatively affect the employer.

An environment that induces negative emotions affects our empathetic brains, causing these negative emotions to spread, 'infecting' entire teams. Consequently, the emotional health of the workplace is very important not only for the individual, but for the whole group. It is also important to note that positive emotions such as happiness can be contagious in the same manner. It is therefore paramount to employee wellbeing and organisational productivity that companies take the idea of a positive workplace seriously.

My Dyslexia – Real Life Case Study F

Name: Lara S
Profession: Deaf Signer
Years in Role: 15

What are your strengths?
- Thinking out of the box.
- Knowing that there is always a way, and I just need to look in the right place.
- Passion.

What are your weaknesses?
- Thinking too much.
- Looking for perfection.
- Lists.
- I would like to be better at research and processing technical knowledge.

What are the best things about being dyslexic/neuro-diverse?
- Connecting to others who are the same, as it makes the world a less lonely place.
- Brainstorming with others of the same mindset.

What are your top three strategies that help you work better? Anything at all! These can be practical, models, psychological.
- Keeping things organised.
- Using my phone for notes.
- Writing everything down!

Chapter 13

A Workplace Guide

The following is a short summary that you might want to show your employer or print out for colleagues who may have also have dyslexia or neurodiversity.

What are some of the issues dyslexic employees face at work?

According to the British Dyslexia Association, the TUC (Trade Union Congress) and many leading dyslexic practitioners:

- Many dyslexic employees experience disciplinary and misconduct-led approaches for problems which are actually disability-related.

- High levels of bullying, stress and mental health problems arise from misunderstanding and poor management of dyslexia and dyspraxia at work.

- In the workplace, there is a limited understanding of reasonable adjustments and what does and doesn't work to resolve performance issues.

- Employers typically find out about dyslexia-related problems via disciplinary measures and grievances.

- Individuals report fear of disclosure because of victimisation by the employer or bullying by workmates.

What You Need to Know as an Employer

Dyslexia is recognised under the Equality Act 2010. Employers have a duty to make *'reasonable adjustments'* to make sure disabled staff are not put at a substantial disadvantage by employment arrangements or any physical features of the workplace. The key to these adjustments is that they are *anticipatory in nature.* This means they should be in place from the start, and not only when they are asked for. Examples of adjustments include:

- Providing modified equipment

- Making instructions and manuals more accessible

- Providing a reader

- Being flexible about working hours – allowing the individual to have different core working hours and to be away from the office for assessment, treatment or rehabilitation

- Providing employees with dyslexia with quiet areas to work where possible

- Providing training or coaching

What You Need to Know as an Employee

It is important to have support from those around you, but there are also things that you, as a dyslexic employee, can do to minimise the difficulties you experience as a result of your neurodiversity. For example:

- Use a 'Do not disturb' sign or inform colleagues that you are unavailable unless it is an emergency. Managing disruptions in this way will help give you the space to concentrate without interruption.

- If you are interrupted, don't be afraid to say, 'I will be with you in five minutes,' and then finish what you were doing. Also, make a note of anything that you are thinking of, which you might need to refer to later. This will save you time when it comes to remembering what you were doing.

- Make a note of all appointments and deadlines in *one* place. This will save you from looking for it later and will ensure that you see *everything* you need to do when you check your planner.

- Finish the day by writing a to-do list for the next day. Doing this whilst information is still clear in your mind will limit the chance of you forgetting to do something important.

Dyslexia can be a major cause of stress for an individual. There are many reasons for this. It could be that the individual is struggling to cope with the workload because they have to re-do and re-check things, which takes longer than their colleagues. It could be that time pressure or pressure from management is causing the person to make more mistakes, at which point their strategies go out the window. It could be that the person has a fear of being 'found out', which can cause its own constant stress.

You can help your employee by sharing some of the following tips.

Talk to Someone

The lonelier and more isolated you feel, the greater your vulnerability to stress. Talking with someone, therefore, can be a great stress relief. This can be your manager, a colleague or someone in a different department. Talking with someone can help calm your nervous system and relieve stress, which builds up from hiding. The other person doesn't have to 'fix' your problems. He or she just has to be a good listener. Sharing your feelings with someone you trust can be very cathartic, even if there is nothing that can be done to alter the stressful situation.

'My colleagues support and understand my dyslexia which helps me carry out my role knowing I have backing from the organisation.'
– Quote from a site services manager.

You never know. By talking about it, you might find that others are also feeling the same about some aspect of their work, and perhaps you can help each other to work more effectively.

Get Some Coaching

A lot of people are sceptical about coaching and often think, 'What can a coach do that hundreds of pounds of technology and training can't?'. The answer is simple. Coaching gives you time to think and it makes it personal to you.

Sometimes the simplest things can solve a problem, yet we choose to over-complicate matters. What's more is that the technology, training and strategies that are assigned to you might have worked for other people with similar difficulties but will not work for you. This is not uncommon. What coaching does is allow you to figure out where your strengths lie and how you can use these to create your own strategies which will work for you.

Manage Your Time

Rushing, being late and not having time will add to your stress. Yes, it is common for dyslexic individuals to have personal organisational challenges, including time management. Follow these simple tips to avoid adding extra time pressure:

- **Leave earlier in the morning.** Leaving even 10-15 minutes earlier in the morning can make the difference between frantically rushing to make the train and having an enjoyable morning, wake up stroll. Ask yourself these questions:

What time do I need to be there?
What time will it be if I arrive 10 mins early?
How long is the journey? (Add in extra for transport delays)
How long will it take to get to my transport?
What time should I leave the house?
How long will it take to get ready?
So what time should I get up?

- **Plan regular breaks.** Make sure you take short 5-10 minute breaks throughout the day to stand up, take a walk, or just do something unrelated to work. Stepping away from work, even for a moment, gives you time to relax and recharge and stops pressure from building up. As a result, you will be more productive and able to deal more calmly with pressure, when you get back to work.

- **Don't over-commit yourself.** Avoid scheduling things back to back, because things always take longer than planned. Also, remember that it is okay to say no! If you feel you won't have the time, or that you will have to delay something that matters to you, then don't do it.

Think Positively

Never underestimate the power of positive thinking! Repetitive, positive thinking and positive activity can rewire your brain and strengthen the brain areas that stimulate positive feelings. Consider restructuring your thoughts as follows:

Negative Self-Talk	Positive Thinking/Action
I've never done that before.	This project is an exciting opportunity to learn a new skill.
It's too complicated.	I just need to look at it from a different angle and apply that creativity I know I have.
There's no way this will work.	I will make it happen!
I will never get this done on time.	I still have 2 days; all I need is a solid plan of action. What's my first step?
No one communicates in this office.	I am going to send John and April an email and see where they are with the project.
I don't have the knowledge or skills to do this.	This is a great opportunity for me to learn something new and to grow professionally.

When your state of mind is generally optimistic, you're better able to handle everyday stress in a more constructive way.

Concentrate on Your Strengths

Sit down and write down your top five strengths. Now ask yourself, 'How can I use these in my role?' and 'Which of these can help me compensate for my dyslexia?' If you can't think of five strengths, ask someone! This can be a friend, colleague or manager, but pick someone who has worked with you and can give you specific examples.

Identifying your strengths will give you a little boost of confidence when times are tough. Moreover, reminding yourself of what you are good at can often give you a new perspective that enables you to approach the stressful situation or task with a clearer and more positive outlook.

Increase Your Psychological Confidence

Increasing your confidence is easier said than done, I know. You are probably thinking, 'If I could do that, I wouldn't have any problems,' and of course you are right. I am not suggesting you can magically be more confident. However, you can *trick* yourself into feeling more confident, particularly for a specific event, like a presentation. Here are a few ways you can do this:

- **Power posing** – Reduces feelings of anxiety and increases confidence levels. Doing this for just two minutes before a presentation can help you feel more positive and confident in your presentation.

- **Smiling** – Releases dopamine, endorphins and serotonin, making you feel more confident. Moreover, our brains have 'mirror neurons', which mimic the emotions of other people – the more you smile. the more your audience will too.

- **Engage in positive thoughts** – Just engaging in 'cognitive reappraisal' (reminiscing about something positive or happy after a stressful event) can reduce cortisol by 15%. Get thinking about that holiday or happy event, smile and feel the stress melt away.

Establish a Good Work-Life Balance

Avoid reading emails at home and reinforce this by not sending any yourself. This promotes mental recovery and means you will come into work rested and feeling the best you can.

Structure Your Ideas When Presenting

Even if you happen to touch upon something of interest, your audience is likely to switch off if you start jumping from point to point, never finishing one train of thought. Here are a few things to think about:

- Include an introduction to help ease in the listener. Engage them by giving them a little preview of what you will talk about.

- Next, talk through the 'main body' of your presentation. Explain the product and its benefits, or why you're right for the job. Try to stick to three to five main points. You do not want to overwhelm the audience.

- Have a solid finish. Summarize the key points and finish on something positive or inspiring: a story, a quote, or a fun fact. Make it memorable.

To help you with this, explore using the PROVE model:

- **P**osition – start with your position or main point

- **R**eason – outline one to three of your most compelling reasons

- **O**ther View – outline how you have considered opposing points of view

- **V**erify – consider what evidence you have for your viewpoint

- **E**nd – summarise the key points and next steps

Be You

You might worry that you are 'different' from those around you. Perhaps you do not do X or Y as well as your colleagues. It is important to be aware that EVERYONE works differently. We are all unique and will all have different preferences, strengths and weaknesses. The important thing is to understand this and to rely on one another's abilities to work effectively as a team. What can you and your company do to accomplish this?

1. Understand yourself, how you like to work and what frustrates you.

2. Encourage your colleagues to do the same and to share their preferences.

3. Encourage everyone to share their strengths and weaknesses. You never know, what may be hellish for you might be enjoyable to others. For example, you might dislike completing spreadsheets and enjoy the meeting clients whereas your colleague might prefer the opposite. Why not swap and both be happy?

The End or the Beginning?

I hope you have enjoyed this book and that it has given you some new and positive ways of understanding your dyslexia or neurodiversity. I also hope you take away some practical ideas for dealing with your unique challenges personally and professionally. Please feel free to contact me with any additional ideas of your own, or to share your thoughts and experiences. I would love to add these to the second edition.

Thank you to all of my contributors who have helped us understand how dyslexia has affected them and who have shared some great insights.

I hope you are feeling inspired and informed about your dyslexia. I also hope that this book helps you develop some effective strategies for things that you see as weaknesses, but more importantly, that it gives you a greater understanding of your dyslexic strengths. Among the thousands of clients I have met, I have seen such great potential and genius (some realised, some not yet).

Thank you to all past clients and hello to new ones. Thank you for letting me be a part of your lives, being such an inspiration and allowing me to have had such a wonderful and fascinating career.

Cheryl Isaacs *B.A. (Hons), M.Sc. C.Psychol, AFBPsS*
Chartered Psychologist (BPS)
Registered Psychologist (HCPC)
Neurodiversity Expert

Ideas or Feedback?

I would love to hear your ideas, tips and strategies and to put them into a second version of this book to help others. Write to me at Cheryl@opmconsulting.co.uk and I would be delighted to include them next time.

Made in the USA
San Bernardino, CA
09 June 2020